THIS BOOK

BELONGS TO

....

....

I can't tell you how grateful I am that you decided to read my book. My most heartfelt thanks that you took time out of your life to choose my work and I hope you find benefit within these pages.

There are so many books available today that offer similar content so that makes it even more humbling that you decided to buying mine.

Tell me what you thought! I am eager to hear your opinion and ideas on what you read as are others who are looking for a good book to buy. Leave a review on Amazon.com so others can benefit from your wisdom!

With much thanks.

Contents

The Critters you'll encounter in this volume are:

Scarf disguised as a snake

Cat Wrap
A copycat to wear around town

Owl Bag
A project for children: easy and fun to knit!

Alligator Scarf
The one and only world-famous gator wrap

Little cousin to the big one

Gator Mittens
A must-have pair for small gator enthusiasts

Loon Backpack
Classy way to tote your stuff around

Lobster Mittens
With moveable claws and sized for kids' hands

Natural accessory for above mittens

Pony Tail Hat
If hair is too short to sport a pony tail

RatRace Scarf
For the modern way of life

Sporting bright red spikes

SUMMARY

Knitter's With Animal Lovers Knitting: Knitter's With Animal Lovers Knitting is a community or group that brings together individuals who have a passion for both knitting and animals. This group provides a platform for like-minded individuals to connect, share their love for knitting, and discuss their mutual adoration for animals.

The members of Knitter's With Animal Lovers Knitting are not only avid knitters but also animal enthusiasts. They find joy in creating beautiful and intricate knitted items while also advocating for the well-being and protection of animals. This group serves as a space where they can combine their two passions and find support and inspiration from others who share their interests.

One of the main objectives of Knitter's With Animal Lovers Knitting is to promote the use of animal-friendly materials in knitting projects. Members are encouraged to use cruelty-free yarns and fibers, such as plant-based or synthetic options, instead of animal-derived materials like wool or silk. This emphasis on ethical knitting aligns with the group's overall mission of respecting and caring for animals.

In addition to promoting animal-friendly knitting practices, Knitter's With Animal Lovers Knitting also aims to raise awareness about animal welfare issues. Members actively engage in discussions and share information about animal rights, adoption, and responsible pet ownership. They may organize events or fundraisers to support local animal shelters or rescue organizations, using their knitting skills to create items that can be sold or donated to raise funds.

The group also serves as a valuable resource for its members. Knitters of all skill levels can seek advice, tips, and patterns from fellow members who have experience in knitting for animals. Whether it's knitting cozy blankets for shelter animals or crafting adorable sweaters for beloved pets, the group offers a wealth of knowledge and inspiration to help members create meaningful and practical items for animals in need.

Knitter's With Animal Lovers Knitting is not just a community; it's a community with a purpose. By combining their love for knitting and animals, members of this group are able to make a positive impact on the lives of animals while indulging in their creative passion. Whether it's through their knitting projects, advocacy efforts, or support for animal welfare organizations, these individuals are united by their shared dedication to both knitting and animals.

The Charm of Integrating Animal Designs into Knitting: The charm of integrating animal designs into knitting is truly captivating and adds a unique touch to any knitted project. Incorporating animal motifs into knitting patterns allows for endless creativity and personalization, making each piece truly one-of-a-kind.

One of the most appealing aspects of integrating animal designs into knitting is the ability to bring nature to life through yarn. Whether it's a cute bunny, a majestic lion, or a playful dolphin, these animal designs can evoke a sense of joy and whimsy. Knitting enthusiasts can create adorable stuffed animals, cozy sweaters, or even intricate blankets that showcase their favorite creatures.

The process of integrating animal designs into knitting requires careful attention to detail and a keen eye for color and texture. Knitters must carefully select the right yarn colors to accurately represent the animal's fur or feathers. Additionally, incorporating different knitting techniques, such as intarsia or fair isle, can help bring out the intricate details of the animal design.

Animal designs in knitting also offer a wonderful opportunity to learn and practice new knitting techniques. From creating intricate cable patterns to mastering the art of duplicate stitch, knitters can expand their skills while bringing their favorite animals to life. This integration of creativity and technical skill is what makes knitting with animal designs so rewarding.

Furthermore, knitting with animal designs can also be a meaningful way to express one's love and appreciation for animals. Whether it's knitting a baby blanket adorned with adorable elephants for a new arrival or crafting a hat with a wolf motif for a nature enthusiast, these knitted creations can serve as heartfelt gifts that celebrate the beauty of the animal kingdom.

In addition to the aesthetic appeal, integrating animal designs into knitting can also have a practical purpose. For example, knitting a hat with animal ears can provide warmth and whimsy for a child during the winter months. Similarly, knitting a scarf with a snake pattern can add a touch of playfulness to an otherwise ordinary accessory.

Overall, the charm of integrating animal designs into knitting lies in the endless possibilities it offers for creativity, skill development, and personal expression. Whether it's a small accessory or a larger project, knitting with animal designs allows knitters to infuse their love for animals into their craft. The result is a truly unique and captivating piece that showcases both their knitting prowess and their admiration for the natural world.

Preparing for Your Knitting for Animal Scarves, Hats, and Mittens:

Knitting is a wonderful and versatile craft that allows you to create beautiful and functional items. If you have a love for animals and want to combine your passion for knitting with your love for furry friends, then knitting animal scarves, hats, and mittens is the perfect project for you.

Before you start knitting, it's important to gather all the necessary materials. You will need a set of knitting needles, preferably in a size suitable for the yarn you will be using. Choose a soft and warm yarn in various colors to bring your animal creations to life. Additionally, you may want to have a pair of scissors, a tapestry needle for weaving in ends, and stitch markers to help you keep track of your progress.

Once you have your materials ready, it's time to choose the animal you want to knit. There are countless options available, from cute and cuddly animals like cats and dogs to more exotic creatures like elephants and giraffes. You can find knitting patterns for animal scarves, hats, and mittens online, in knitting books, or even create your own design.

Before you start knitting, it's important to familiarize yourself with the knitting pattern. Read through the instructions carefully, noting any special stitches or techniques that may be required. Make sure you understand the abbreviations used in the pattern, as they will guide you through the knitting process.

Next, you will need to cast on your stitches. This is the process of creating the foundation row of stitches on your knitting needle. The number of stitches you cast on will depend on the size of the animal scarf, hat, or mitten you are making. Follow the pattern instructions for the correct number of stitches.

Once you have cast on your stitches, you can begin knitting. Follow the pattern instructions row by row, working the specified stitches and techniques. Pay attention to any shaping instructions, such as increasing or decreasing stitches, to create the desired shape of your animal creation.

As you knit, it's important to keep track of your progress. Use stitch markers to mark important points in the pattern, such as the beginning of a round or the placement of certain stitches. This will help you stay organized and ensure that your animal scarf, hat, or mitten turns out just as you envisioned.

Once you have completed all the rows and stitches specified in the pattern, it's time to finish off your knitting.

Selecting Yarns: Types, Colors, and Textures of Animal Knitting and Hats and Mittens Knitting: When it comes to selecting yarns for your knitting projects, there are several factors to consider, including the types, colors, and textures available. This is especially true when it comes to animal knitting and knitting hats and mittens.

Firstly, let's discuss the types of yarns that are commonly used for these types of projects. Animal knitting typically involves using yarns made from natural fibers such as wool, alpaca, or mohair. These fibers are known for their warmth and durability, making them perfect for creating cozy animal-themed garments. On the other hand, when it comes to knitting hats and mittens, you have a wider range of options. While natural fibers are still popular choices, you can also opt for synthetic yarns like acrylic or nylon, which offer different benefits such as being more affordable or easier to care for.

Next, let's talk about the colors available for your knitting projects. Animal knitting often involves using earthy tones such as browns, grays, and whites to mimic the natural colors of the animals being represented. This creates a realistic and visually appealing finished product. However, you can also experiment with brighter colors to add a fun and whimsical touch to your animal knits. When it comes to hats and mittens, the color options are virtually endless. You can choose from a wide range of vibrant hues to match your personal style or to create eye-catching accessories that stand out in a crowd.

Lastly, let's delve into the textures of yarns that can be used for these projects. Animal knitting often requires yarns with a fluffy or fuzzy texture to mimic the fur of the animals being represented. This adds depth and dimension to your knits, making them look more lifelike. For hats and mittens, you have more flexibility in terms of texture. You can choose smooth and sleek yarns for a polished and classic look, or opt for chunky and textured yarns to create a more cozy and rustic feel.

In conclusion, selecting yarns for animal knitting and knitting hats and mittens involves considering the types, colors, and textures available. Natural fibers like wool, alpaca, and mohair are commonly used for animal knitting, while a wider range of options exists for hats and mittens. Earthy tones are often used for animal knits, but you can also experiment with brighter colors. The textures of yarns can vary depending on the project, with fluffy or fuzzy yarns being popular for animal knitting,…

Essential Tools for Knitting: When it comes to knitting, having the right tools is essential for a successful and enjoyable experience. Whether you are a beginner or an experienced knitter, having a well-stocked knitting toolkit will ensure that you have everything you need to create beautiful and intricate designs. Here are some of the essential tools for knitting that every knitter should have in their collection.

1. Knitting Needles: Knitting needles are the most basic and fundamental tool for knitting. They come in various sizes and materials, such as metal, wood, or plastic. The size of the needles you choose will depend on the thickness of the yarn you are using and the desired tension of your project. It is recommended to have a range of needle sizes in your collection to accommodate different projects.

2. Yarn: Yarn is the main material used in knitting, and having a variety of yarns in different colors, textures, and weights will allow you to create a wide range of projects. From soft and cozy wool to lightweight and breathable cotton, there are endless options to choose from. It is important to select yarns that are suitable for the type of project you are working on, as different yarns have different properties and characteristics.

3. Stitch Markers: Stitch markers are small rings or clips that are used to mark specific stitches or sections in your knitting. They are particularly useful when working on complex patterns or when shaping your project. Stitch markers come in various sizes and styles, and they can be easily moved along the knitting needles as you progress in your project.

4. Scissors: A good pair of scissors is essential for cutting yarn and trimming loose ends. It is important to have a dedicated pair of scissors for your knitting projects to avoid damaging the blades or using them for other purposes. Choose a pair of scissors that are sharp and comfortable to hold, as you will be using them frequently throughout your knitting journey.

5. Tape Measure: Accurate measurements are crucial in knitting, especially when it comes to sizing garments or determining the length of your project. A tape measure is a handy tool that allows you to measure your knitting accurately. Look for a tape measure that is flexible and easy to read, with both metric and imperial measurements.

6. Stitch Holders: Stitch holders are used to hold stitches that are not currently being worked on. They come in various shapes and sizes, such as straight or safety pin-like designs.

Organizing and Caring for Your Knitting Supplies: Organizing and caring for your knitting supplies is essential for any avid knitter. Not only does it help keep your materials in good condition, but it also ensures that you can easily find what you need when starting a new project. Whether you are a beginner or an experienced knitter, having a well-organized knitting space can greatly enhance your knitting experience.

First and foremost, it is important to have a designated area for your knitting supplies. This can be a small corner in your living room, a spare room, or even a portable knitting bag if you prefer to knit on the go. Having a dedicated space allows you to keep all your supplies in one place, making it easier to find and access them whenever you want to knit.

Once you have your knitting space set up, it's time to organize your supplies. Start by sorting your yarns by color, weight, or project type. This will make it easier to find the perfect yarn for your next project. You can use clear plastic bins or baskets to store your yarn, making it visible and easily accessible. Additionally, consider investing in yarn organizers or shelves to keep your yarn neatly arranged and prevent it from tangling.

Next, organize your knitting needles and crochet hooks. You can use a needle case or a roll-up organizer to keep them in one place. Sort them by size or type, and label each compartment accordingly. This will save you time and frustration when searching for the right needle or hook for your project.

Don't forget about your knitting notions and accessories. These include stitch markers, tapestry needles, measuring tapes, and scissors, among others. Keep them in a small container or pouch, so they are easily accessible when needed. You can also use a magnetic strip or a pin cushion to store your stitch markers, ensuring they don't get lost.

Proper care of your knitting supplies is equally important. Always store your yarn in a cool, dry place to prevent it from getting damaged by moisture or pests. Avoid exposing your yarn to direct sunlight, as it can cause fading or discoloration. If you have pets, make sure to keep your yarn and needles out of their reach to prevent any accidents.

Regularly clean your knitting needles and crochet hooks to remove any dirt or residue. You can use a mild soap and warm water to gently clean them. Dry them thoroughly before storing them to prevent rusting.

Understanding and Following Knitting Patterns: Understanding and following knitting patterns is an essential skill for any knitter, whether you are a beginner or an experienced crafter. Knitting patterns provide a roadmap for creating beautiful and intricate designs, and being able to decipher and execute them accurately is crucial for achieving the desired results.

To begin with, it is important to have a basic understanding of the terminology and abbreviations commonly used in knitting patterns. These can vary from pattern to pattern, but there are some universal terms that every knitter should be familiar with. For example, "k" stands for knit, "p" stands for purl, and "yo" stands for yarn over. Additionally, there are abbreviations for different types of stitches, such as "k2tog" for knit two stitches together and "ssk" for slip, slip, knit.

Once you have a grasp of the terminology, the next step is to carefully read and analyze the pattern instructions. Knitting patterns are typically divided into sections, with each section detailing a specific part of the project. It is important to read through the entire pattern before starting, as this will give you an overview of the project and help you understand how the different sections fit together.

When reading the instructions, pay close attention to any special notes or tips provided by the designer. These can often contain valuable information that will make the knitting process easier and more efficient. Additionally, take note of any stitch counts or measurements mentioned in the pattern, as these will help ensure that your finished project turns out the correct size.

One of the most important aspects of following a knitting pattern is understanding the stitch pattern or chart. This is typically represented by a series of symbols or diagrams that indicate which stitches to knit or purl in each row. It is crucial to carefully study and interpret the stitch pattern, as any mistakes or misinterpretations can result in a flawed design. If you are unsure about any part of the stitch pattern, it is always a good idea to consult a knitting reference book or seek guidance from more experienced knitters.

In addition to understanding the stitch pattern, it is also important to pay attention to the gauge specified in the pattern. Gauge refers to the number of stitches and rows per inch, and it is crucial for ensuring that your finished project matches the dimensions specified in the pattern. To achieve the correct gauge, it may be necessary to adjust your needle size or tension.

Tips and Tricks for Adding Character to for Animal Scarves, Hats, and Mittens Knitting:

When it comes to knitting animal scarves, hats, and mittens, adding character is what makes them truly special and unique. Whether you're knitting for yourself or for someone else, incorporating fun and whimsical elements can bring these accessories to life. Here are some tips and tricks to help you add character to your animal-themed knitting projects.

1. Choose the Right Yarn: The type of yarn you use can greatly impact the overall look and feel of your animal accessories. Opt for yarns that have a soft and fluffy texture, as they will give your creations a more cuddly and adorable appearance. Consider using yarns with different colors or variegated patterns to add depth and dimension to your animal designs.

2. Use Embroidery Techniques: Embroidery can be a fantastic way to add intricate details and features to your animal scarves, hats, and mittens. You can use embroidery stitches to create eyes, noses, mouths, and other facial features. Experiment with different embroidery techniques, such as satin stitch, backstitch, or French knots, to achieve

the desired effect. Don't be afraid to get creative and add unique embellishments like sequins or beads for extra sparkle.

3. Incorporate Appliqué: Appliqué is another technique that can add character to your animal-themed knitting projects. By attaching fabric or knitted pieces onto your accessories, you can create additional details like ears, paws, or tails. Consider using contrasting colors or patterns for the appliqué pieces to make them stand out and add visual interest.

4. Experiment with Different Stitch Patterns: The stitch pattern you choose can also contribute to the overall character of your animal accessories. For example, using a cable stitch can create a textured effect that resembles fur or scales. Alternatively, you can try using a popcorn stitch to add a bumpy texture that mimics animal skin. Play around with different stitch patterns to find the ones that best represent the animal you're trying to recreate.

5. Add Accessories: To further enhance the character of your animal scarves, hats, and mittens, consider adding small accessories or embellishments. For example, you can attach buttons as eyes or use ribbons to create bows or collars. These little details can make a big difference in bringing your animal creations to life.

Adapting Patterns for Different Sizes and Preferences for Animal Scarves, Hats, and Mittens Knitting:

When it comes to knitting animal scarves, hats, and mittens, one size does not fit all. Different individuals have varying sizes and preferences, and it is important to adapt patterns accordingly to ensure a perfect fit and meet their unique style choices.

To begin with, adapting patterns for different sizes requires understanding the measurements of the person or animal for whom the item is being knitted. For scarves, the length and width can be adjusted based on the wearer's height and personal preference. For hats, the circumference and depth should be tailored to fit the head snugly without being too tight or loose. Mittens, on the other hand, need to be customized to fit the hand size and finger length of the wearer.

To adapt patterns for different sizes, it is essential to have a good understanding of knitting techniques and the ability to modify stitch counts and shaping. For example, if a pattern calls for a certain number of stitches for a scarf, increasing or decreasing the stitch count can be done to achieve the desired width. Similarly, for hats and mittens, adjusting the number of stitches in the initial rounds can help achieve the right size.

In addition to size, preferences also play a significant role in adapting patterns. Animal scarves, hats, and mittens come in various designs, ranging from cute and whimsical to realistic and detailed. Some individuals may prefer a scarf with a longer tail or a hat with larger ears, while others may opt for a more subtle and minimalistic design. Adapting patterns to meet these preferences involves modifying the stitch patterns, color choices, and embellishments used in the knitting process.

When adapting patterns for different sizes and preferences, it is important to keep in mind the overall balance and proportion of the finished item. For example, if a scarf is being lengthened, it is crucial to ensure that the tail does not become too heavy or disproportionate to the rest of the scarf. Similarly, when modifying the design of animal hats, it is important to maintain the integrity of the animal's features while accommodating the wearer's preferences.

In conclusion, adapting patterns for different sizes and preferences in knitting animal scarves, hats, and mittens requires careful consideration of measurements, knitting techniques, and design choices. By understanding the unique needs and style choices of the wearer, one can create customized items that fit perfectly and reflect their individuality.

Washing, Drying, and Storing Your Animal Scarves, Hats, and Mittens Knitting: When it comes to caring for your beloved animal scarves, hats, and mittens knitting, it is essential to follow proper washing, drying, and storing techniques to ensure their longevity and maintain their quality. By taking the time to care for these items correctly, you can enjoy them for years to come.

Firstly, before washing your animal scarves, hats, and mittens knitting, it is crucial to check the care instructions provided by the yarn manufacturer. Different types of yarn may require specific washing methods, such as hand washing or machine washing on a gentle cycle. Following these instructions will help prevent any damage or distortion to the knitted items.

If hand washing is recommended, fill a basin or sink with lukewarm water and add a mild detergent suitable for delicate fabrics. Gently submerge the animal scarves, hats, and mittens knitting into the water, making sure they are fully saturated. Avoid agitating or wringing the items, as this can cause stretching or felting. Instead, gently squeeze the soapy water through the fabric to remove any dirt or stains.

After washing, rinse the items thoroughly with clean water to remove any soap residue. Again, avoid wringing or twisting the knitted pieces. Instead, gently press out the excess water by squeezing them between your hands or rolling them in a clean towel. This will help retain their shape and prevent any stretching.

When it comes to drying your animal scarves, hats, and mittens knitting, it is best to lay them flat on a clean, dry towel or a mesh drying rack. Avoid hanging them, as this can cause them to stretch or lose their shape. Reshape the items if necessary, gently pulling them back into their original form. Allow them to air dry completely before storing or wearing them again.

Proper storage is essential to protect your animal scarves, hats, and mittens knitting from dust, moths, and other potential damage. Before storing, ensure that the items are completely dry to prevent any mildew or mold growth. It is recommended to store them in a clean, dry, and well-ventilated area, away from direct sunlight and excessive heat.

To further protect your knitted items, consider using acid-free tissue paper or cotton fabric to wrap them individually. This will help prevent any color transfer or snagging. Additionally, storing them in airtight containers or zip-lock bags can provide an extra layer of protection against dust and pests.

Regularly inspect your animal scarves

Minor Repairs and Refinishing Worn Knits for Animal Scarves, Hats, and Mittens Knitting:

When it comes to knitting animal scarves, hats, and mittens, it's not uncommon for these adorable creations to experience some wear and tear over time. Whether it's a loose stitch, a small hole, or simply a worn-out appearance, these minor issues can detract from the overall charm and functionality of these knitted accessories. That's where our expertise in minor repairs and refinishing comes in.

At our knitting studio, we specialize in breathing new life into worn knits, particularly those featuring animal designs. Our skilled artisans have years of experience in knitting and are well-versed in the intricacies of repairing and refinishing knitted items. We understand the sentimental value attached to these unique pieces, and we take great care in restoring them to their former glory.

When you bring your animal scarves, hats, or mittens to us for repair or refinishing, our first step is to carefully assess the damage. We examine each stitch, identifying any loose threads, holes, or areas of wear. This meticulous inspection allows us to develop a comprehensive plan for restoration, ensuring that every issue is addressed.

For minor repairs, we employ various techniques to fix loose stitches or mend small holes. Our artisans use specialized tools and high-quality yarn to seamlessly blend the repaired areas with the rest of the knit. We pay close attention to the original pattern and design, ensuring that the repaired sections are virtually indistinguishable from the rest of the piece.

In cases where the wear and tear are more extensive, we offer refinishing services. This involves carefully unraveling the damaged sections and reknitting them to match the original design. Our artisans have a keen eye for detail and are skilled in recreating intricate animal patterns, ensuring that the finished product looks as good as new.

Throughout the repair or refinishing process, we maintain open communication with our clients. We understand that these knitted accessories often hold sentimental value, and we want to ensure that our clients are involved in the restoration process. We provide regular updates, seeking approval for any design choices or alterations that may be necessary.

Once the repairs or refinishing are complete, we take the time to carefully inspect the finished product. We ensure that every stitch is secure, every pattern is intact, and every detail is in place.

Ensuring the Longevity of Your Handmade Pieces for Animal Scarves, Hats, and Mittens Knitting: Ensuring the longevity of your handmade animal scarves, hats, and mittens knitting is essential if you want to enjoy your creations for years to come. Handmade pieces require extra care and attention to maintain their quality and durability. By following a few simple tips and tricks, you can ensure that your knitted items remain in excellent condition and withstand the test of time.

First and foremost, it is crucial to choose the right materials for your knitting projects. Opt for high-quality yarns that are specifically designed for durability. Look for yarns that are made from natural fibers such as wool or alpaca, as these materials are known for their strength and longevity. Avoid using synthetic yarns, as they tend to wear out more quickly and may not hold up well over time.

When it comes to knitting techniques, consider using reinforced stitches for areas that are prone to wear and tear, such as the edges of scarves or the fingertips of mittens. Reinforced stitches, such as slip stitches or duplicate stitches, add an extra layer of strength to your knitted fabric, making it more resistant to fraying or unraveling.

Proper blocking and finishing techniques are also essential for maintaining the longevity of your handmade pieces. Blocking refers to the process of shaping and stretching your knitted item to its desired dimensions. This step helps to even out the stitches and give your piece a polished look. Follow the blocking instructions provided with your yarn or consult knitting resources for guidance on how to block your specific project.

Additionally, finishing techniques, such as weaving in loose ends and securing seams, are crucial for preventing unraveling and maintaining the overall integrity of your knitted items. Take the time to carefully weave in any loose ends using a tapestry needle, ensuring that they are securely fastened. Similarly, reinforce seams by using a strong yarn or thread and double stitching if necessary.

Proper care and storage are also vital for preserving the longevity of your handmade pieces. Always follow the care instructions provided with your yarn, as different fibers require different care methods. Hand wash your knitted items using a gentle detergent and lukewarm water, and avoid wringing or twisting them to remove excess moisture. Instead, gently squeeze out the water and lay your items flat to dry, reshaping them if necessary.

Packing and Presenting Animal Scarves, Hats, and Mittens Knitting as Gifts: When it comes to packing and presenting animal scarves, hats, and mittens knitting as gifts, attention to detail and creativity can make all the difference. These adorable and cozy accessories are not only practical but also serve as a fashion statement, making them the perfect gift for animal lovers of all ages.

To begin with, selecting the right packaging materials is crucial. Opt for high-quality gift boxes or bags that are sturdy enough to protect the knitted items during transportation. Consider choosing packaging that complements the animal theme of the accessories, such as boxes with paw prints or bags with cute animal illustrations. This will add an extra touch of charm and excitement to the gift.

Next, carefully fold and arrange the scarves, hats, and mittens to showcase their unique animal designs. Take the time to ensure that each item is neatly folded and free from any wrinkles or creases. For scarves, consider folding them in a way that highlights the animal face or pattern, allowing the recipient to immediately recognize the adorable creature. For hats and mittens, arrange them in a way that showcases their animal features, such as ears or paws.

To add a personal touch, consider including a handwritten note or card expressing your well wishes and the thought behind the gift. This will make the recipient feel special and appreciated. You can also attach a small tag or label to each item, indicating the type of animal it represents. This will not only add a decorative element but also make it easier for the recipient to identify and enjoy their new accessories.

If you want to take the presentation to the next level, consider adding some additional elements to the packaging. For example, you can include a small plush toy or figurine of the animal that matches the accessories. This will not only enhance the overall theme but also provide the recipient with a cute keepsake to cherish. Another idea is to include a small packet of hot chocolate or a tea bag with an animal-themed label, allowing the recipient to enjoy a warm beverage while wearing their new knitted accessories.

Lastly, don't forget to consider the occasion and the recipient's preferences when choosing the packaging and presentation style. For a birthday or holiday gift, you can add festive ribbons or bows to make the packaging more celebratory. If the recipient has a favorite animal, try to incorporate that specific animal into the packaging design or include a small trinket related to their favorite creature.

In conclusion, packing and presenting animal scarves, hats, and mittens knitting as gifts

Caterpillar Scarf

This squiggly wiggly project is ideal for using up odd skeins of yarn. Although the pattern is written for worsted weight yarn, you can substitute slightly thinner yarn. And if you are lucky enough to have a ball of slightly slippery yarn in your stash in a bug-appropriate shade, use it! Your gauge might be a little different, but gauge on a scarf is not that crucial – go by feel: if it feels soft, squishy and wiggly, it will be perfect for this Scarf.

Knit the Caterpillar in two colors as I did on the samples, or knit each ridge in a different color for an exceptionally cheerful-looking Caterpillar. If you want to make the scarf longer than 50" (127 cm), add one pattern repeat each of **Pattern A** and **Pattern B** and for a wider scarf, increase stitches to 24 or more stitches in **Pattern A** and to 22 stitches in **Pattern B**.

Size: About 50" (127 cm) long from head to tip of tail and 5" (12.7 cm) wide at its widest.

Yarn: Worsted weight yarn in 2 colors (main color and contrast color), 150 yards (137 m) per color. Samples are knit with Morehouse Merino 3-Strand.

Other Material: Small piece of white wool felt for eyes, white sewing thread.

Needle: US 7 or 8 (4.5 mm or 5 mm), use larger needles if you knit tight; you'll also need a crochet hook size C or D (2.75 mm or 3.25 mm) for eyebrows.

Gauge: 15 stitches = 4" (10 cm) over garter stitch pattern.

Start at the head of the Caterpillar Scarf. Cast on 8 stitches with contrast yarn color. Knit 1 row. Next, increase 1 stitch at the beginning of each row until you have 20 stitches total (work increases as follows: knit first stitch, but don't drop stitch off left-hand needle; now knit stitch again, this time through back of stitch). Knit 14 rows. Then *knit row to last 2 stitches, knit those 2 stitches together; repeat from * until you have 10 stitches left. Break off yarn and switch to main yarn color. Knit 2 rows then start with **Pattern A**.

PATTERN A

Increase 1 stitch at the beginning of each row (work increase the same as before) until you have 20 stitches. Knit 14 rows. Then *knit row to last 2 stitches, knit those 2 stitches together; repeat from * until you have 10 stitches left. Knit 2 rows. Work **Pattern A** a total of 4 times. Then start with **Pattern B**.

PATTERN B

Increase 1 stitch at the beginning of each row until you have 18 stitches. Knit 12 rows. Then *knit row to last 2 stitches, knit those 2 stitches together; repeat from * until you have 8 stitches left. Knit 2 rows. Work **Pattern B** a total of 3 times.

TAIL

Switch to contrast yarn color. Knit 2 rows. Increase 1 stitch at the beginning of each row until you have 16 stitches. Knit 12 rows. Then *knit row to last 2 stitches, knit those 2 stitches together; knit 2 rows. Repeat from * until you have 2 stitches left. Bind off.

EYES

Cut out two felt circles for eyes approximately the size of an American penny (about 2 cm) and sew on head using sewing thread (check picture for positioning of eyes). Then crochet two eyebrows right over the eyes with yarn double and using chain stitch (check pictures). You might prefer to crochet the eyebrows first, then sew on the eyes.

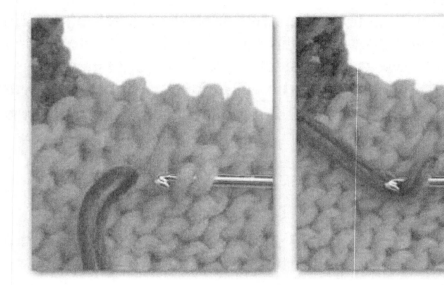

Kissing Fish Mittens

What's so irresistible about these mittens? The bright red kissing lips are the attraction! Use a sturdy piece of wool felt and double it (see instructions below) for plenty of lip smacking. And if you have enough yarn left over, keep it in a safe place for the inevitable emergency and tears when one of the mittens goes AWOL and a new mate is needed ASAP. Or if you have the time, knit a third mitten now and keep it in a safe place.

Children Sizes: Small 5"length (12.7 cm), medium 6" (15 cm) and large 7" (17.7 cm).

Yarn: Multi-colored worsted weight yarn in a "fishy" color combination, approximately 140 yards (128 m). Sample pair is knit with Variegated Morehouse Merino 3-Strand in FantaSea.

Other Materials : Piece of red wool felt, 4" x 4" (10 cm x 10 cm); small piece of yellow felt for eyes; 2 tiny beads for middle of eyes; sewing thread to match felt colors.

Needles : Set of double-pointed US 4 or 5 (3.5 mm or 3.75 mm) or size to obtain gauge.

Notions : 2 stitch markers, small stitch holder or paper clip.

Gauge: 5 stitches = 1"(2.5 cm) over stockinette stitch.

CUFF

Cast on 26 (30/34) stitches. Join for knitting in the round and knit 16 (18/20) rounds or desired length for cuff (if you want to roll up edge of cuff, add 8 rounds). If you prefer a ribbed cuff, work the 16 (18/20) rounds in 1x1 rib pattern as follows: *knit 1 stitch, purl 1 stitch; repeat from * to end of round.

THUMB GUSSET

Start thumb gusset in next round: knit 1 stitch, place first stitch marker, increase 1 stitch (work increase as follows: with left-hand needle pick up yarn between stitches; then knit through back of loop over needle so stitch will be twisted), knit 1, increase 1, place second marker, knit to end of round. Knit 2 rounds. Repeat these three rounds – increasing after the first and before the second marker in the first round, then followed by 2 knit rounds – until you have 7 (9/11) stitches between markers. End thumb gusset with the 2 knit rounds. Next round: knit 1, place the next 7 (9/11) stitches on stitch holder (or paper clip), then knit to end of round – pull yarn tight after that first stitch to avoid gap where you put stitches on holder.

TIP

Knit 20 (23/26) rounds. Then start decreases. Next 2 rounds: *knit 2 stitches together; repeat from * to end of rounds (ending rounds with knit 1) = 7 (8/9) stitches left. Bind off remaining stitches (there will be a small opening at top of mittens that will be covered by the felt lips).

THUMB

Put stitches from holder on three needles. Pick up 2 stitches between first and last stitch. Knit 10 (12/14) rounds. Next round: *knit 2 stitches together, repeat from * to end of round. Pull yarn through remaining stitches.

Knit the second mitten same as the first one.

KISSING LIPS

Cut out felt: 4 pieces each of lips and 4 round eyes. Lips should measure 1½"width (3.8 cm) at bottom edge and eyes should be about ½" (1.3 cm) in diameter. With sewing thread, sew 2 lips together along curves only (see illustration below). Then sew lips to mitten tip – covering hole at bind-off. Add bead to middle of eyes (use sewing thread double), then sew eyes on mittens.

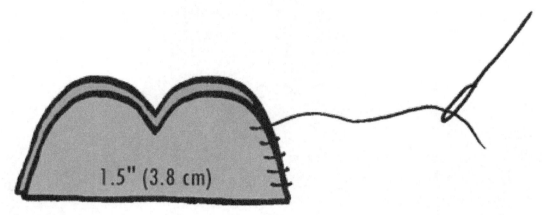

1.5" (3.8 cm)

Sew onto mittens along this edge

Gecko Scarf

The wizard of lizards enjoys a wide circle of friends and fans. And if you count a loved one among those fans (or if you are one yourself), this Scarf will be the crème de la crème of groupie attire.

Instead of using two yarn colors and knitting stripes on the body of the Gecko, you could substitute a multi-colored yarn (with lots of green in it?) and ignore instructions for stripes. Another way to make your Gecko super special is by adding a shiny bead to each tip of its toes. Tiny, shiny claws on a Gecko… très chic!

Tip: If the instructions for the eyelids sound too complicated, you can simply ignore them and knit 20 rows, then pick up the pattern again beginning with *Finishing Head*. And instead of cutting out circles for eyes, cut two semi-circles of felt.

Size: From nose to tip of tail about 58" (147 cm) long and 7½" (19 cm) wide.

Yarn: Sport weight yarn in 2 colors (color A & B), 225 yards (206 m) each color. Samples are knit with Morehouse Merino 2 Ply.

Other Material: Small piece of bright green wool felt for eyes; sewing thread to match color of felt.

Needles: Set of double-pointed US 4 or 5 (3.5 mm or 3.75 mm) or size to obtain gauge. Gecko Scarf is knit back and forth, but you'll need extra needles for eyelids and toes.

Gauge : 20 stitches = 4" (10 cm) over garter stitch.

Start with the head of the Gecko. Cast on 8 stitches with yarn color A. Knit 1 row. Next, increase 1 stitch at the beginning of each row until you have 35 stitches total (work increases as follows: knit first stitch, but don't drop stitch off left-hand needle; now knit stitch again, this time through back of stitch). Knit 18 rows.

EYE LIDS

They'll look like sideways pockets where you'll insert the felt eyes later. Divide stitches over three double-pointed needles: the first 5 stitches on first needle, the next 25 stitches on the second needle, and the last 5 stitches on third needle. Now knit the first 5 stitches, then (using a new needle) knit the next 25 stitches on second needle. Turn and continue knitting the middle 25 stitches – knit a total of 14 rows. Break off yarn, leaving a 10" tail. With new needle, cast on 5 stitches then add (by knitting) the 5 stitches on third needle (by knitting them in following order: stitch #31 first, followed by stitch #32, #33, etc. to end of row). Knit 14 rows on these 10 stitches. Break off yarn, leaving a 10" tail. With new needle, cast on 5 stitches. With wrong side of knitting facing you, add (by knitting) the stitches from first needle (by knitting them in following order: knit stitch #5 first, followed by stitch #4, then stitch #3, etc. to beginning of row). Knit 14 rows on these 10 stitches. The next picture illustrates what it will look like.

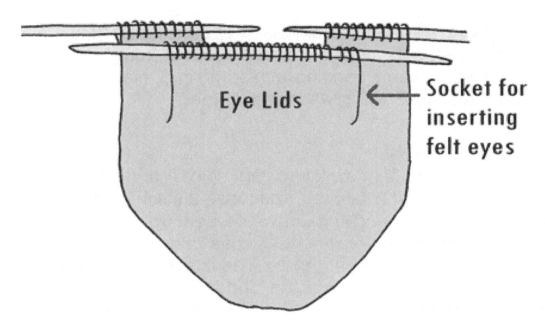

Cast-on stitches create flaps on wrong side

Eye Lids

Socket for inserting felt eyes

Knit next row as follows (right side facing you): knit the first 5 stitches on first needle; now put second needle parallel to first needle (with second needle in front – closest to you) and knit the first 5 stitches on second needle together with the remaining 5 stitches on first needle (similar to three-needle bind-off – except you don't bind off stitches). Knit the next 15 stitches on second needle and knit the remaining 5 stitches together with first 5 stitches on third needle. Then knit the remaining 5 stitches on third needle. You now have 35 stitches again – all on one needle. Knit 5 additional rows.

FINISHING HEAD

Finish head as follows: * knit row to last 4 stitches, knit the next 2 stitches together, then knit the last 2 stitches. Knit 2 rows. Repeat from * until you have 31 stitches left, ending with 2 knit rows.

BODY

Increase 1 stitch at beginning of next 4 rows (work increases the same way as on head) = 35 stitches. *Switch to yarn color B and knit 2 rows. Then knit 2 additional rows and increase 1 stitch at the beginning of each row= 37 stitches. Switch back to yarn color A and knit 2 rows. When switching yarn colors for stripes, don't break off yarn, just pull up new yarn color loosely at side. Next: *knit 4 rows in yarn color B, then 2 rows in yarn color A; repeat from * until you have 41 stripes in yarn color B, ending with stripe in B. Next: knit 2 rows in yarn color A followed by 2 rows in yarn color B.

TAIL

Start to decrease for tail: *switch to yarn color A and knit 2 rows, knit the next 2 rows to last 2 stitches, knit those 2 stitches together. Switch to yarn color B and knit 2 rows. Repeat from * until you have 10 thin stripes in yarn color B = 19 stitches remaining. Break off yarn color B and finish tail with yarn color A as follows: *knit 6 rows, knit the next 2 rows to last 2 stitches, knit those 2 stitches together. Repeat from * until you have 3 stitches left. Next: knit first stitch, knit the last 2 stitches together. Bind off first stitch and pull yarn through remaining stitch.

LEFT FEET

With right side facing you and head of Gecko at top, pick up 15 stitches at left side of body with yarn color B beginning at 5th stripe on body (37th stripe for hind leg). Pick up stitches toward tail and pick up 1 stitch per 2 rows. Knit 1 row. Next: *Knit row (right side); on next row (wrong side) increase 1stitch at beginning of row, then knit row to last 2 stitches, knit those 2 stitches together; repeat from * for a total of 16 rows (stitch count will remain at 15). Next we'll create an elbow – the bend in the leg: *knit row to last 2 stitches, knit those 2 stitches together; repeat from * until you have 10 stitches left. Knit next (wrong side) row. Next row: *increase 1 stitch at beginning of row, knit row to last 2 stitches, knit 2 stitches together; knit 1 row. Repeat from * for a total of 12 rows (stitch count will remain at 10).

TOES

For first toe, use the first 3 stitches and put them on a separate needle. Then knit 6 rounds of I-cord (see below how to knit I-cord); pull yarn through stitches. For second toe, put the next 2 stitches on a separate needle and increase 1 stitch between the two stitches. Then knit 6 rounds of I-cord and pull yarn through stitches. For third toe, repeat instructions for second toe. And for last toe, use remaining 3 stitches and repeat instructions for first toe.

How to knit I-cord: knit the 3 stitches on needle. Then slide stitches to other end of needle and knit the stitches again in the same stitch sequence as in first row – pulling yarn tight between last stitch and first stitch on new row.

RIGHT FEET
Pick up 15 stitches at same stripe location as feet on other side – mark spot on body where feet ended on left side, because this time you'll be picking up stitches towards head. Knit first row (wrong side). Next row: *increase 1 stitch at beginning of row, knit row to last 2 stitches, knit those 2 stitches together. Knit next row. Repeat from * for a total of 16 rows. Next row: *knit row to last 2 stitches, knit those 2 stitches together. Repeat from * until you have 10 stitches left. Knit next row (wrong side). Knit 1 more row (right side). Next row: *increase 1 stitch at beginning of row, knit row to last 2 stitches, knit those 2 stitches together. Knit next row. Repeat from * for a total of 12 rows. Work toes the same way as toes on left feet.

FELT EYES
Sew eye socket pockets on wrong side so they form pockets to slide eyes into. Then cut out 2 slightly oval-shaped circles for eyes. Insert felt eyes into sockets and sew to edge of eyelid. If you skipped the eye lids, cut out 2 semi circles and sew on head.

Bear Paw Mittens

Black bear, brown bear, grizzly or polar bear – any bear-colored yarn will work for this pair. And if you have been putting mitten-knitting on hold because double-pointed needles intimidate you, the Bear Paws might just be the start of your exploration into mitten territory. They are knit back and forth the long way, thumb is knit right onto mitten and the only scary (only mildly so) thing about this pattern is the three-needle bind-off. Go for it!

I'm including an adult size, because once you make a pair you might want to start knitting these mittens by the dozens – with or without claws! The pattern lends itself easily to adaptations: to accommodate longer fingers add stitches above thumb, for a longer cuff add still more stitches but this time below thumb, and for wider hands add rows. And if plain garter stitch mittens don't cut it, embellish them with felt (flowers or shapes similar to Henry Matisse's paper cut-outs), buttons, pompoms, creative stitching, etc.

Tip: If you want to keep going with the bear theme, add a "Honey-dipped Scarf". You'll find the instructions for the Scarf at the end of the Mitten pattern.

Sizes: Child small 5"length (12.7 cm), child medium 6" (15 cm), child large 7" (17.7 cm), and adult 8" (20.3 cm).

Yarn: Bear-colored worsted weight yarn, from 120 to 160 yards, depending on size (109 to 146 m). Sample pair is knit with Morehouse Merino 3-Strand in BrownHeather.

Other Materials : Piece of yellow wool felt, 4" x 4" (10 cm x 10 cm); sewing thread to match felt color.

Needles : US 4 or 5 (3.5 mm or 3.75 mm) or size to obtain gauge (you'll need three needles for three-needle bind-off).

Gauge: 20 stitches = 4" (10 cm) over garter stitch.

The Bear Paw Mittens are knit the long way (or sideways): from wrist to tip of finger on the front of the hand and over to the back of the hand back down to wrist, all in one piece. Cast on 54 (60/70/84) stitches and knit 28 (30/34/36) rows. Next, knit to middle of row: 27 (30/35/42) stitches and put the two needles parallel to each other. With third needle, start binding off stitches together from both needles (that's called three-needle bind-off). Here is how: knit first stitch from needle closest to you together with first stitch on needle in back (knit them as one stitch), then knit second stitch on needle closest to you together with second stitch on needle in back, then bind off regularly by lifting first stitch over second one.

Continue this way – knitting 2 stitches together from front and back needle – binding off a total of 12 (14/18/22) stitches. Count stitches as you are binding them off, not as you are knitting them. You are, of course, binding off double that number of stitches, since you are binding off stitches from front and back needle simultaneously.

THUMB

Now knit the next 4 (5/6/7) stitches off needle in front, turn and knit 5 (6/7/8) stitches (this count includes the last stitch from bind off), pick up 1 stitch between bind off and stitches on back needle, then knit the next 4 (5/6/7) stitches from back needle. Turn and knit these 10 (12/14/16) stitches for thumb. Knit a total of 16 (18/20/22) rows. Next, knit 5 (6/7/8) stitches to middle of row, put needles parallel to each other and bind off the stitches from needle in front and back using three-needle bind-off again. Break off yarn. Re-attach yarn at bottom of thumb and bind off remaining stitches for cuff (again, bind off stitches together from needle in front and needle in back using three-needle bind-off). Make second mitten.

Before sewing sides of mitten together, add felt claws.

FELT CLAWS

Cut out two claws. Fold in middle (you might have to use a steam iron to create a fold) and sew along fold to top of mitten with sewing thread. Fold claws together and sew both sides together along each claw. Sew mitten together (with left-over yarn): along side of thumb and back side of mitten.

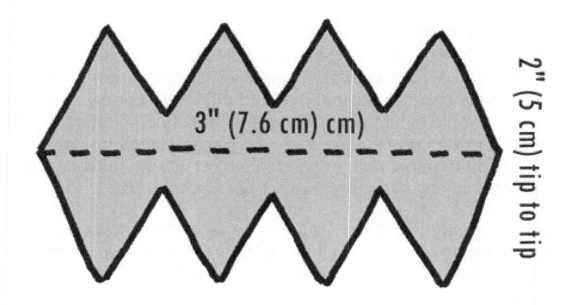

3" (7.6 cm) cm)

2" (5 cm) tip to tip

MITTEN STRING

Use yarn double and crochet or braid string 34" (86 cm) long and attach ends to mittens at thumb side. I do not recommend adding string to mittens for children under 3 years.

HONEY-DIPPED SCARF

Want to knit more bear-themed accessories? How about a scarf with fringe that looks like Goldilocks or one of the three bears got the tips of their scarf caught in the honey pot.

Size: About 7" (17.7 cm) wide and 48" (122 cm) long.

Yarn: Worsted weight in bear color, 150 yards (137 m), small amount of yellow yarn for fringe.

Needles: US 11 (8 mm), crochet hook for pulling fringe through edge of scarf.

Gauge: 12 stitches = 4" (10 cm) over garter stitch.

Cast on 20 stitches and knit until scarf measures between 48" and 54" (122 cm and 137 cm) or whatever length you'd like it to be (for a small child 48" is long enough). Bind off. Then use honey-colored (yellow) yarn and add fringe. For each fringe use 3 pieces of yarn about 12" long. Fold fringe yarn in half and pull middle loop through edge of scarf (with crochet hook), then pull fringe ends through loop and pull tight to fasten. Braid or crochet fringe to half total length of yarn, then tie knot.

Critter Scarves:
Raccoon, Cats & Fox

A charming foursome, perfect for outfitting an entire outdoor-loving family. The idea for these Critter Scarves came to me after looking at an old photograph of a fashionably-clad lady wrapped in a fox stole. Today we are much luckier (never mind the fox and raccoon!), we can knit a warm and cozy version of that stole that's totally guilt-free and animal- and eco-friendly (and a lot more likeable!).

Variations can include stripes over entire body (on my critters, only the tails are striped) and stitched whiskers and noses on cat's faces. Or knit an all-black or dark-brown version and you've got a mink or a ferret. And if you want longer scarves, add additional rows to the body and/or add an inch or two to the tail.

Tip, Trip or Tripe: For the body of the Critter you get to knit 240 rows without color change or stitch variations… some of you might call this stretch boredom, I call it bliss! It's my favorite kind of knitting. Time to daydream, plan a vacation or tomorrow's menu, watch TV or the birds outside the window. I savor every single stitch! Look at those 240 rows as an opportunity to enjoy the company of your own thoughts, dreams and fantasies. Hey – it's a suggestion!

Size: About 48" long (122 cm) from tail to tip of nose.

Yarn: Sport weight yarn in two contrasting colors, one light and one dark, 225 yards (205 m) per color; small amount of yarn in brown, dark grey or black for tip of nose. Samples are knit with Morehouse Merino 2-Ply.

Other Materials : Small piece of yellow felt for eyes; sewing thread to match felt color and black thread or yarn for stripes in eyes.

Needles : Set of double-pointed US 4 or 5 (3.5 mm or 3.75 mm) or size to obtain gauge.

Gauge: 20 stitches = 4" (10 cm) over garter stitch.

TAIL

Start your Critter at the tip of the tail and cast on 5 stitches with light yarn color. Knit 2 rows. Next: *increase 1 stitch (work increases as follows: knit first stitch, but don't drop stitch off left-hand needle; now knit stitch again, this time through back of stitch) at beginning of the next 2 rows, then knit 2 rows; repeat from * until you have 13 stitches. *Switch to dark yarn color and knit 2 rows. Back to light yarn color and increase 1 stitch at the beginning of next two rows. Repeat from * until you have 21 stitches; switching yarn colors every 2 rows (don't break off yarn after knitting the 2 rows, just let it hang at side of knitting, then pull it up loosely when you are ready to start with that yarn color again). Next: *knit 2 rows with light yarn color, then 2 rows with dark yarn color; repeat from * until tail measures about 15"(38 cm) from tip (if you want tail be longer, add a few more stripes), ending with stripe in dark yarn color. Keep stripe pattern intact and work the next 6 rows as follows: knit row to last 2 stitches, knit those 2 stitches together; ending with stripe in light yarn color and 15 stitches on needle. Break off light yarn color (leave piece of yarn long enough to darn in).

BODY

Continue with dark yarn color for body of critter. Knit 1 row. Work next row as follows: *knit 1 stitch, increase 1 stitch (work increases as follows: with left-hand needle, pick up yarn between stitches; then knit through back of loop over needle); repeat from * to end of row, ending with knit 1. You now have 29 stitches. Knit 1 row. Next row: knit 15 stitches, increase 1 stitch, knit to end of row = total of 30 stitches on needle. Knit 240 rows for body (or more if you want a longer scarf). Knit next row as follows: knit first stitch, *knit 2 stitches together; repeat from * to end of row, ending row with knit 1 = 16 stitches remaining. Knit 1 more row. Break off dark yarn color.

HEAD
Switch to light yarn color and use yarn double. Entire head is knit with yarn double (you'll be knitting with 2 strands of yarn held together). Knit and increase 1 stitch at the beginning of the next 10 rows (work increases same as on tail) = 26 stitches on needle.

Raccoon Critter only: switch to dark yarn color and use yarn double and knit 10 rows. Switch back to light yarn color (again, use yarn double) and knit 2 additional rows.

Cat & Fox Critters only: knit 14 rows.

Finish head as follows (*on all Critters*): *knit row to last 2 stitches, knit those last 2 stitches together; repeat from * until you have 6 stitches left. Switch to small piece of yarn for nose, using yarn double, and knit next row as follows: *knit 2 stitches together; repeat from * to end of row. Knit next row. Increase 1 stitch at the beginning of next 2 rows. Then bind off as follows: knit 2 stitches (bind off first stitch), knit the next 2 stitches together (and bind off second stitch), then knit remaining 2 stitches and bind them off.

EARS
With light yarn color (use yarn single for ears, not double as for head), cast on 2 stitches. Increase 1 stitch at the beginning of the next 10 rows (work increases same as on tail) = 12 stitches on needle. Knit 6 rows. Bind off. Make a second ear. Fold ear (see picture) and sew to side of head.

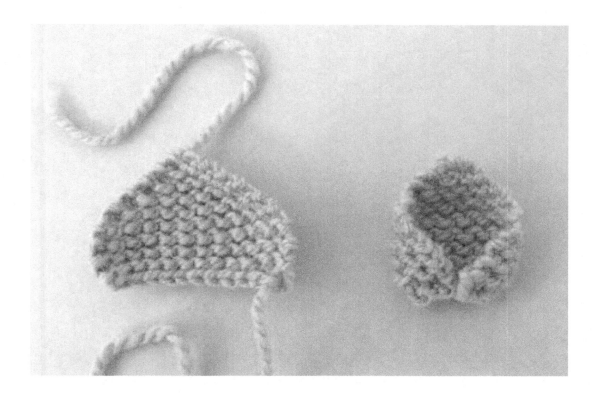

EYES

Cut out felt circle about ¾" (about 2 cm) in diameter. With black sewing thread or yarn, stitch a line through middle of circle (or you can use a sewing machine – cut felt into a 1-inch ribbon, then sew a line along the middle of strip with zig-zag stitches as close together as possible, then cut out circles). Sew eyes on head with sewing thread.

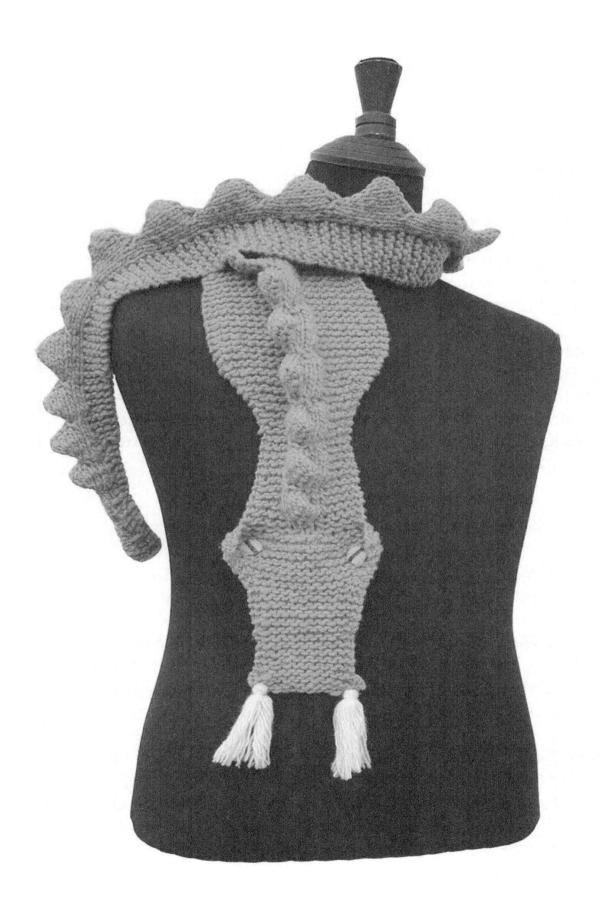

Dragon Scarf

Legendary creature, figment of our imagination, or stitched together with real wool by a real-life knitter, Dragons are fascinating beasts. Despite its spiky appearance, this Dragon Scarf is a loveable companion on frosty days.

Tip: My Dragon is puffing smoke or steam, whichever. If you want a fire-breathing Dragon, use yellow/orange yarn for those tassels spewing from the nostrils.

A Note about this Pattern: Don't let the length of it discourage you. The Dragon Scarf is not a difficult project. The fact that almost every row is a little different and that I wanted the pattern to be absolutely clear, added to the length of it – and not the complexity of the design. Once you get the hang of knitting those spikes, the pattern rolls off the needles effortlessly.

Size: 62 "long (157 cm); width varies from head to tail.

Yarn: Worsted weight yarn, 290 yards (265 m). Sample is knit with Morehouse Merino 3-Strand in GreenTomato.

Other Materials : Small piece of yellow felt for eyes; sewing thread to match felt color and black thread or yarn for stripes in eyes. Small amount of lace yarn or fingering weight yarn for smoke or fire "breath" of Dragon.

Needles : US 6 or 7 (4.25 mm or 4.5 mm) or size to obtain gauge (you'll need 3 needles for three-needle bind-off); crochet hook for pulling "breath" fringe through edge of nostril on Dragon.

Gauge: 16 stitches = 4" (10 cm) over garter stitch.

3 STEPS THAT YOU'LL BE REPEATING THROUGHOUT THIS PATTERN

Step 1: Knit to middle stitch and increase 1 stitch before middle stitch, knit middle stitch, then increase 1 stitch after middle stitch. Knit to end of row. Work increases as follows: with left-hand needle, pick up yarn between stitches; then knit through back of loop over needle. By knitting into the back of the loop over needle, you'll be twisting the stitch you are knitting and thus avoid creating a hole where you worked the increase.

Step 2, the Spike Row: Knit to middle stitch. Knit middle stitch using third needle – now bind off, using three-needle bind-off as follows: put the two needles with stitches parallel to each other and knit the first stitch on needle closest to you together with first stitch on needle in back. Bind off. Next, knit second stitch on needle closest to you together with second stitch on needle in back and bind off. Bind off the required number of stitches (pattern will state: bind off 3, 4 or 5 stitches – actually you are binding off double that number because you are knitting two stitches together before binding them off; make sure you count stitches as you are binding them off, not as you are knitting them), then put stitch on third needle back onto needle in right hand and knit to end of row.

Step 3: Increase 1 stitch at the beginning of row (between first and second stitch), knit to middle stitch, increase 1 stitch before middle stitch, knit middle stitch and increase 1 stitch after middle stitch; then knit row to last stitch and increase 1 stitch before last stitch, then knit last stitch. **Tip:** You'll be working this row after **Spike Row** and you may want to work increase before middle stitch by picking up yarn between stitches from row below instead of the row you are on, because the bind-off for the **Spike Row** creates a small gap and by working the increase a row deeper, you can close that gap a little.

TAIL AND BODY

Start at tail end and cast on 5 stitches. *Knit 10 rows. Next row: increase 1 stitch each at the beginning and at the end of the row. Increase between first and second stitch and before last stitch. Repeat from * once more. *Knit next row (right side) and work next row (wrong side) as follows: knit 3 stitches, purl 3 stitches, knit 3 stitches. Repeat from * once more. Mark middle stitch with a piece of different color yarn.

PLEASE NOTE: the numbers below are *not* row counts, but indicate order of steps to be worked.

Start Spike pattern.

1. Right Side (abbreviated RS): work **Step 1.**

2. Wrong Side (abbreviated WS): knit 3 stitches, purl to last 3 stitches, knit the last 3 stitches.

Repeat these 2 rows until you have 17 stitches, ending with a WS row.

3. RS: work **Step 2, the Spike Row**. Bind off 3 stitches (a total of 6 stitches). You'll have 11 stitches left.

4 . WS: knit 3 stitches, purl to last 3 stitches, knit 3.

5. RS: work **Step 3**.

6. WS: knit 4, purl to last 4 stitches, knit 4.

7. RS: repeat **Step 1.**

8. WS: knit 4, purl to last 4 stitches, knit 4.

Repeat these last 2 rows until you have a total of 21 stitches, ending with a WS row.

9. RS: repeat **Step 2, the Spike Row**, but this time bind off 4 stitches (a total of 8 stitches).

10. WS: knit 4, purl to last 4 stitches, knit 4.

11. RS: repeat **Step 1.**

12. WS: knit 4 stitches, purl to last 4 stitches, knit 4 stitches.

Repeat these last 2 rows until you have 23 stitches, ending with a WS row.

13 . RS: repeat **Step 2, the Spike Row**, but this time bind off 5 (a total of 10 stitches)

14. WS: knit 4 stitches, purl to last 4 stitches, knit 4 stitches.

15. RS: repeat **Step 3.**

16. WS: knit 5 stitches, purl to last 5 stitches, knit 5.

17. RS: *repeat **Step 1.**

18. WS: knit 5 stitches, purl to last 5 stitches, knit 5.

Repeat these last 2 rows until you'll have a total of 25 stitches, ending with a WS row.

19. RS: repeat **Step 2, the Spike Row**, bind off 5 (a total of 10 stitches).

20. WS: knit 5 stitches, purl to last 5 stitches, knit 5.

Repeat from * (repeat steps 17 through 20).

21. RS: repeat **Step 3.**

22. WS: knit 6 stitches, purl to last 6 stitches, knit 6.

23. RS: *repeat **Step 1.**

24. WS: knit 6 stitches, purl to last 6 stitches, knit 6.

Repeat these last 2 rows until you have a total of 27 stitches, ending with WS row.

25. RS: repeat **Step 2, the Spike Row**, bind off 5 (a total of 10 stitches).

26. WS: knit 6 stitches, purl to last 6 stitches, knit 6.

Repeat from * (steps 23 through 26).

27. RS: repeat **Step 3.**

28. WS: *knit 7 stitches, purl to last 7 stitches, knit 7.

29. RS: repeat **Step 1.**

30. WS: knit 7 stitches, purl to last 7 stitches, knit 7.

Repeat these last 2 rows until you have a total of 29 stitches, ending with WS row.

31. RS: repeat **Step 2, the Spike Row**, bind off 5 (a total of 10 stitches).

Repeat from * two more times (you'll have worked steps 28 through 31 a total of three times).

32. WS: knit 7 stitches, purl to last 7 stitches, knit 7.

33. RS: repeat **Step 3.**

34. WS: *knit 8 stitches, purl to last 8 stitches, knit 8.

35. RS: repeat **Step 1.**

36. WS: knit 8 stitches, purl to last 8 stitches, knit 8.

Repeat these last 2 rows until you have a total of 31 stitches, ending with WS row.

37. RS: repeat **Step 2, the Spike Row**, bind off 5 (total of 10).

Repeat from * two more times (you'll have worked steps 34 through 37 a total of three times).

38. WS: knit 8 stitches, purl to last 8 stitches, knit 8.

39. RS: repeat **Step 3.**

40. WS: *knit 9 stitches, purl to last 9 stitches, knit 9.

41. RS: repeat **Step 1.**

42. WS: knit 9 stitches, purl to last 9 stitches, knit 9.

Repeat these last 2 rows until you have a total of 33 stitches, ending with WS row.

43: RS: repeat **Step 2, the Spike Row**, bind off 5 (a total of 10 stitches).

Repeat from * two more times (you'll have worked steps 40 through 43 a total of three times).

44. WS: knit 9 stitches, purl to last 9 stitches, knit 9.

45. RS: repeat **Step 3.**

46. WS: *knit 10 stitches, purl to last 10 stitches, knit 10.

47. RS: repeat **Step 1.**

48. WS: knit 10 stitches, purl to last 10 stitches, knit 10.

Repeat these last 2 rows until you have a total of 35 stitches, ending with WS row.

49. RS: repeat **Step 2, Spike Row**, bind off 5 (a total of 10 stitches).

Repeat from * (steps 46 through 49).

50. WS: knit 10 stitches, purl to last 10 stitches, knit 10.

51. RS: repeat **Step 3.**

52. WS: knit 11 stitches, purl to last 11 stitches, knit 11.

53. RS: repeat **Step 1.**

54. WS: knit 11 stitches, purl to last 11 stitches, knit 11.

Repeat these last 2 rows until you have a total of 37 stitches, ending with WS row.

55. RS: repeat **Step 2, Spike Row**, bind off 5 (a total of 10 stitches).

56. WS: knit 11 stitches, purl to last 11 stitches, knit 11.

57. RS: repeat **Step 3.**

58. WS: knit 12 stitches, purl to last 12 stitches, knit 12.

59. RS: repeat **Step 1.**

60. WS: knit 12 stitches, purl to last 12 stitches, knit 12.

Repeat these last 2 rows until you have a total of 39 stitches, ending with WS row.

61. RS: repeat **Step 2, Spike Row**, bind off 5 (a total of 10 stitches).

62. WS: knit 12 stitches, purl to last 12 stitches, knit 12.

63. RS: repeat **Step 3.**

64. WS: knit 13 stitches, purl to last 13 stitches, knit 13.

65. RS: *repeat **Step 1.**

66. WS: knit 13 stitches, purl to last 13 stitches, knit 13.

Repeat these last 2 rows until you have a total of 41 stitches, ending with WS row.

67. RS: repeat **Step 2, Spike Row**, bind off 5 (a total of 10 stitches).

68. WS: knit 13 stitches, purl to last 13 stitches, knit 13.

Repeat from * (steps 65 through 68).

69. RS: **Step 4** (this is a new procedure, you'll be using it in this and subsequent rows): knit the first 2 stitches together, then knit to middle stitch, increase 1 stitch before middle stitch, knit middle stitch, increase 1 stitch, knit row to last 2 stitches, knit those 2 stitches together.

70. WS: knit 12, purl to last 12 stitches, knit 12.

71. RS: repeat **Step 4.**

72. WS: knit 11, purl to last 11 stitches, knit 11.

73. RS: repeat **Step 4.**

74. WS: knit 10, purl to last 10 stitches, knit 10.

75. RS: repeat **Step 4.**

76. WS: knit 9, purl to last 9 stitches, knit 9.

77. RS: repeat **Step 4.**

78. WS: knit 8, purl to last 8 stitches, knit 8.

79. RS: knit the first 2 stitches together. Then knit to middle stitch and repeat **Step 2, the Spike Row**, bind off 5 (a total of 10 stitches). Knit row to last 2 stitches, knit those 2 stitches together.

80. WS: knit 7, purl to last 7 stitches, knit 7.

81. RS: repeat **Step 4.**

82. WS: knit 6, purl to last 6 stitches, knit 6.

83. RS: repeat **Step 4.**

84. WS: knit 5, purl to last 5 stitches, knit 5.

85. RS: *repeat **Step 1.**

86. WS: knit 5, purl to last 5 stitches, knit 5.

87. RS: repeat **Step 2, the Spike Row**, bind off 4 (a total of 8 stitches).

88. WS: knit 5, purl to last 5 stitches, knit 5.

89. RS: *repeat **Step 1.**

90. WS: knit 5, purl to last 5 stitches, knit 5.

Repeat from * until you have 21 stitches, ending with WS row.

91. RS: repeat **Step 2, the Spike Row**, bind off 4 (a total of 8 stitches).

92. Knit 3 rows.

HEAD

93. RS: *knit 1, increase 1; repeat from * to end of row.

94. WS: knit row.

95. RS: knit 1, increase 1, knit 1, increase 1, knit row to last 2 stitches, increase 1, knit 1, increase 1, and knit last stitch.

96. Knit 3 rows.

97. RS: knit first stitch, *knit 2 stitches together; repeat from * two more times (total of three times), knit row to last 7 stitches, *knit 2 stitches together, repeat from * two more times, knit last stitch.

98. WS: knit row.

99. RS: knit first stitch, *knit 2 stitches together, repeat from *, knit row to last 5 stitches, *knit 2 stitches together, repeat from *, knit last stitch.

100. WS: knit row.

101. RS: *knit first stitch, knit 2 stitches together, knit row to last 3 stitches, knit 2 stitches together, knit last stitch. Knit 1 row. Repeat from * two more times (total of three times). Knit 12 rows. Next row: knit first 2 stitches together, knit row to last 2 stitches, knit those 2 stitches together. Knit 10 rows.

NOSTRILS

*Next row: increase 1 stitch at the beginning and at end of row. Knit 1 row. Repeat from *. Next row: knit the first 2 stitches together, knit row to last 2 stitches, knit those 2 stitches together. Bind off in next row.

SNORT TASSELS

Wrap white lace or fingering yarn around your closed fingers about 20 times. Insert one end of the loops (keep loops together in a bunch) through edge of nostril (use large crochet hook), then pull other end through loop. Pull tight and cut tassel open at other end. Repeat for other nostril.

EYES

Cut out felt circle about ¾" (about 2 cm) in diameter. With black sewing thread or yarn stitch a line through middle of circle (or you can use a sewing machine – cut felt into a 1-inch ribbon, then sew a line along the middle of strip with stitches as close together as possible, then cut out circles). Check picture of eyes in Critter Scarves. Sew eyes on head with sewing thread.

Dragon Hat

Let's top off the Dragon Scarf with a Dragon Hat. Same basic concept for those spikes as in the Dragon Scarf – except that the Hat is knit in the round.

A word about hats and fits: snug-fitting hats are warmer and will provide a better fit in the long run. Knits stretch out, especially ribbed borders. If a hat is knit to the size of an adult's head circumference of around 22" (56 cm), it will soon be too loose to be comfortably warm after some wear and tear. The important thing is to cast on loosely and use an elastic cast-on so hat slips easily over head.

Tip: The Dragon Hat is meant to be the tail of the beast, but that doesn't mean you can't finish it with the same tassel, a k a smoke or fire, that's coming out of the Dragon's nostrils. Let's not be picky!

Sizes: Child medium, child large (or adult small) and adult.

Yarn: Worsted weight yarn, 290 yards (265 m). This Hat gets a little bottom heavy because of its length, use a light-weight worsted yarn. Sample is knit with Morehouse Merino 3-Strand in GreenTomato.

Needles : Set of double-pointed US 5 or 6 (3.75 mm or 4.25 mm) or size to obtain gauge; 1 extra double-pointed needle, same size or smaller, for Spike Rounds. You can start Hat using a 16" (40 cm) circular needle, then switch to double-pointed needles when circumference of Hat gets smaller towards tip.

Notions : Stitch marker.

Gauge: 18 stitches = 4" (10 cm) over stockinette stitch.

Cast on 76 (80/84) stitches. Use an elastic cast-on method (such as long-tail cast-on; and cast on loosely). Join for knitting in the round and mark beginning of round with stitch marker. Next, work 10 (12/12) rounds in 1x1 rib pattern (worked as follows: *knit 1 stitch, purl 1 stitch; repeat from * to end of round). Next round: knit 38 (40/42) stitches (to middle of round), place marker, increase 1 stitch (increase by picking up yarn between stitches with left-hand needle, then knitting through back of loop over needle); knit to end of round. Mark this new middle stitch with a piece of different-color yarn – this stitch will be the ridge stitch on the row of Dragon Spikes = 77 (81/85) stitches. Knit 1 round.

FIRST SPIKE

Round 1: knit to marker, increase 1 stitch (same as before), knit middle stitch, increase 1 stitch,

then knit to end of round = 79 (83/85) stitches.

Round 2: knit.

Round 3: knit to marker, increase 1 stitch, knit 3 stitches, increase 1 stitch, knit to end of round = 81 (85/89) stitches.

Round 4: knit.

Round 5: knit to marker, increase 1 stitch, knit 5 stitches, increase 1 stitch, knit to end of round = 83 (87/91) stitches.

Round 6 : knit.

Round 7 : knit to marker, increase 1 stitch, knit 7 stitches, increase 1 stitch, knit to end of round = 85 (89/93) stitches

Round 8 : knit.

Round 9 : knit to marker, increase 1 stitch, knit 9 stitches, increase 1 stitch, knit to end of round = 87 (91/95) stitches.

Round 10 : knit.

Round 11 (Spike Round): knit to middle stitch. Knit middle stitch using spare needle. Now bind off stitches for spike using three-needle bind-off as follows: put the needle with the stitches you just knit and the needle with the next stitches to be knit, parallel to each other and knit the first stitch on needle closest to you together with first stitch on needle in back. Bind off (using middle stitch). Next, knit second stitch on needle closest to you together with second stitch on needle in back and bind off. Bind off 5 stitches (you are actually binding off double that number of stitches because you are knitting two stitches together for each bind-off stitch; make sure you count stitches as you are binding them off, not as you are knitting them), then put stitch from last bind off (now on spare needle) back onto needle in right hand (this will be your middle stitch again) and knit to end of round = 77 (81/85) stitches. Place marker before middle stitch again.

Round 12 : knit.

These 12 rounds finish the first spike on the Dragon Hat.

SECOND SPIKE
Repeat rounds 1 through 12.

THIRD SPIKE
Repeat Rounds 1 through 11 and work Round 12 as follows: knit 2 (0/2) stitch(es); *knit 2 stitches together, knit 7 (8/8) stitches; repeat from * to middle stitch, place marker before middle stitch then knit middle stitch; *knit 7 (8/8) stitches, knit 2 stitches together; repeat from * to end of round; ending round with knit 2 (0/2) stitch(es) = 69 (73/77) stitches remaining.

FOURTH SPIKE

Repeat Rounds 1 through 11 and work Round 12 as follows: knit 2 (0/2) stitch(es); *knit 2 stitches together, knit 6 (7 (7); repeat from * to middle stitch, place marker before middle stitch then knit middle stitch; *knit 6 (7/7) stitches, knit 2 stitches together; repeat from * to end of round; ending round with knit 2 (0/2) stitch(es) = 61 (65/69) stitches remaining.

FIFTH SPIKE

Repeat Rounds 1 through 11 and work Round 12 as follows: knit 2 (0/2) stitch(es); *knit 2 stitches together, knit 5 (6/6); repeat from * to middle stitch, place marker before middle stitch then knit middle stitch; *knit 5 (6/6) stitches, knit 2 stitches together; repeat from * to end of round; ending round with knit 2 (0/2) stitch(es) = 53 (57/61) stitches remaining.

SIXTH SPIKE

Repeat Rounds 1 through 11 and work Round 12 as follows: knit 2 (0/2) stitch(es); *knit 2 stitches together, knit 4 (5/5) stitches; repeat from * to middle stitch, place marker before middle stitch then knit middle stitch; *knit 4 (5/5) stitches, knit 2 stitches together; repeat from * to end of round; ending round with knit 2 (0/2) stitch(es) = 45 (49/53) stitches remaining.

SEVENTH SPIKE

Repeat Rounds 1 through 11 and work Round 12 as follows: knit 2 (0/2) stitch(es); *knit 2 stitches together, knit 3 (4/4) stitches; repeat from * to middle stitch, place marker before middle stitch then knit middle stitch; *knit 3 (4/4) stitches, knit 2 stitches together; repeat from * to end of round; ending round with knit 2 (0/2) stitch(es) = 37 (41/45) stitches remaining.

EIGHTH SPIKE

Repeat Rounds 1 through 11 and work Round 12 as follows: knit 2 (0/2) stitch(es); *knit 2 stitches together, knit 2 (3/3) stitches; repeat from * to middle stitch, place marker before middle stitch then knit middle stitch; *knit 2 (3/3) stitches, knit 2 stitches together; repeat from * to end of round; ending round with knit 2 (0/2) stitch(es) = 29 (33/37) stitches remaining.

NINTH SPIKE

Repeat Rounds 1 through 11 and work Round 12 as follows: knit 2 (0/2) stitch(es); *knit 2 stitches together, knit 1 (2/2) stitches; repeat from * to middle stitch, place marker before middle stitch then knit middle stitch; *knit 1 (2/2) stitches, knit 2 stitches together; repeat from * to end of round; ending round with knit 2 (0/2) stitch(es) = 21 (25/29) stitches remaining.

TENTH SPIKE

Repeat Rounds 1 through 8 (skip Rounds 9 & 10). Next, work **Spike Row** by binding off 4 stitches, instead of 5. Next, work Round 12 as follows: knit 2 (0/2) stitch; *knit 2 stitches together, knit 0 (1/1) stitch; repeat from * to middle stitch, place marker before middle stitch then knit middle stitch; *knit 0 (1/1) stitch, knit 2 stitches together; repeat from * to end of round; ending round with knit 2 (0/2) stitch = 13 (17/21) stitches remaining.

ELEVENTH SPIKE

Repeat Rounds 1 through 8 (skip Rounds 9 & 10). Next, work **Spike Row** by binding off 4 stitches, instead of 5. Next, work Round 12 as follows: *knit 2 stitches together; repeat from * to middle stitch, place marker before middle stitch then knit middle stitch; *knit 2 stitches together; repeat from * to end of round = 7 (9/11) stitches remaining.

Child Medium Size only: pull yarn through stitches.

Adult and Child Large Sizes: add twelve spike.

TWELFTH SPIKE

Repeat Rounds 1 through 6 (skip Rounds 7 through 10). Work **Spike Row** by binding off 3 stitches, instead of 5. Next, work Round 12 as follows: knit 0 (1) stitch; *knit 2 stitches together; repeat from * to middle stitch, knit middle stitch; *knit 2 stitches together; repeat from * to end of round; ending round with knit 0 (1) stitch. Pull yarn through remaining stitches.

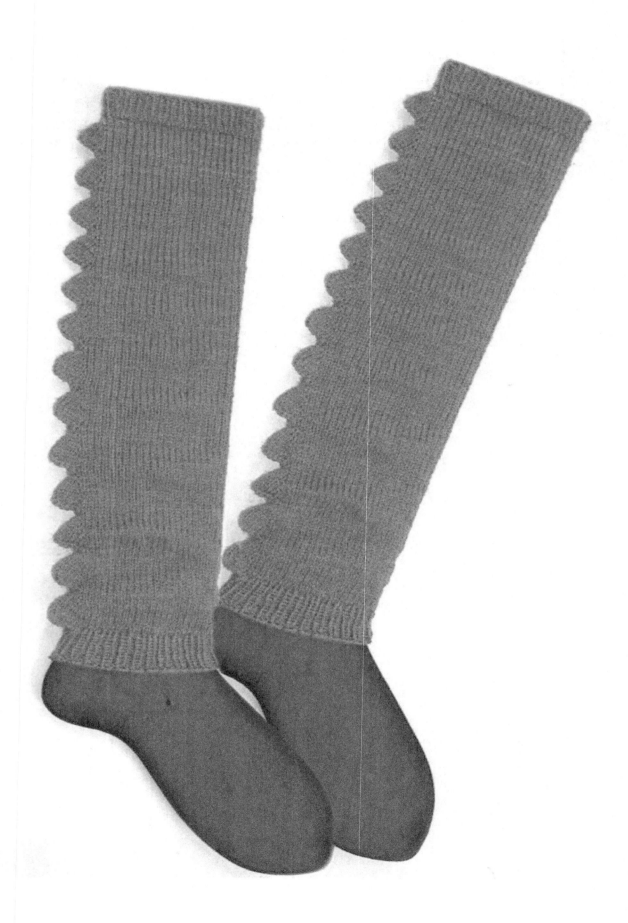

Dragon LegWarmers

We've got the Scarf and the Hat. So let's give this dragon ensemble some legs. The LegWarmers are knit in round with the same spike pattern as the Dragon Scarf and Hat.

Size and length can be adjusted easily. The stitches for the spikes are added at the beginning and end of the round, so you can easily add stitches for wider leg warmers to fit over jeans or delete stitches for spindly legs. And to shorten them, simply omit some of the spikes.

Sizes: Child regular, adult small (or child large), adult regular; up to 22" (56 cm) length.

Yarn: Sport weight yarn, 440 yards (402 m). Sample pair is knit with Morehouse Merino 2-Ply in GreenTomato.

Needles : Set of double-pointed US 3 or 4 (3.25 mm or 3.5 mm) or size to obtain gauge.

Gauge: 24 stitches = 4" (10 cm) over stockinette stitch.

Cast on 48 (52/56) stitches. Use an elastic cast-on method, such as long-tail cast-on, and cast on loosely. Divide stitches over 3 needles instead of 4 (it will be easier to work 3-needle bind-off for spikes if stitches are distributed over 3 needles). Join for knitting in the round and work 10 rounds in 1x1 rib pattern as follows: *knit 1 stitch, purl 1 stitch; repeat from * to end of round.

START SPIKES

Round 1: increase 1 stitch at beginning of round stitch (increase by picking up yarn between stitches with left-hand needle, then knitting through back of loop over needle), knit to end of round = 49 (53/57) stitches.

Round 2: knit.

Round 3: knit first stitch, increase 1 stitch; then knit to end of round and increase 1 stitch at end of round (put this stitch on third needle) = 51 (55/59) stitches.

Round 4: knit.

Round 5: knit 2 stitches, increase 1 stitch; then knit round to last stitch, increase 1 stitch, knit last stitch = 53 (57/61) stitches.

Round 6: knit.

Round 7: knit 3 stitches, increase 1 stitch; then knit round to last 2 stitches, increase 1 stitch, knit the last 2 stitches = 55 (59/63) stitches.

Round 8: knit.

Round 9: knit the first 4 stitches, increase 1 stitch; then knit round to last 3 stitches, increase 1 stitch, knit the last 3 stitches = 57 (61/65) stitches.

Round 10: knit

Round 11: knit the first 5 stitches, increase 1 stitch; then knit round to last 4 stitches, increase 1 stitch, knit the last 4 stitches = 59 (63/67) stitches.

Round 12: knit first stitch, put the first and third needle parallel to each other and work three-needle bind-off as follows: knit next stitch on needle closest to you (on first needle) together with last stitch on needle in back (on third needle), then bind off first stitch; knit next stitch on needle closest to you together with last stitch on needle in back, then bind off second stitch. Continue this way – binding off a total of 5 stitches (you are actually binding off double that number because you are knitting two stitches together before binding them off; make sure you count stitches as you are binding them off, not as you are knitting them). Then knit round to last stitch, knit this last stitch together with first stitch (put stitch on third needle) = 48 (52/56) stitches.

Repeat these 12 rounds a total of 10 to 13 times (to desired length of Dragon Legs).

End LegWarmers with 10 rounds of 1x1 ribbing. Bind off loosely. Make second one.

Chi-Chi Panda Scarf

What's black and white and cuddly cute? Nope, not a penguin, it's a panda bear! The panda is among the world's most adored animals ever since Chi Chi arrived at the London Zoo in 1958 (she was the model for the black and white logo of the World Wildlife Fund and she is lending her name to this Scarf).

I knit my Panda Scarf with Morehouse Merino 2-Ply, a fairly smooth sport weight yarn and I think it ended up looking a little bare instead of fluffy. Black and white fuzzy yarns would work wonders in upping the cute and cuddly factor on this scarf. Hope you got some in your stash! For a longer Panda, simply knit additional rows in the white belly part of the pattern.

Tip: Short little black felt claws at the tip of each foot? Just an idea! I personally think of panda bears as big fluff balls, all cuddly, and way too sweet-tempered to bare claws. But I am probably all wrong!

Size: About 44" long (112 cm) and 7" wide (18 cm).

Yarn: Sport weight yarn, 225 yards (206 m) each in black and white. Sample is knit with Morehouse Merino 2-Ply.

Needles : Set of double-pointed US 4 or 5 (3.5 mm or 3.75 mm).

Notions : Stitch holder or holding needle, same size or smaller than the needles you are knitting with.

Gauge: 20 stitches = 4" (10 cm) over garter stitch (but gauge is not crucial).

The entire Panda Scarf is knit in garter stitch. You start with back legs, then knit body, add front legs and end scarf by knitting the head.

BACK LEGS

With black yarn, cast on 15 stitches. Knit 1 row. Increase 1 stitch at the beginning of next 2 rows (increase by knitting first stitch twice as follows: knit first stitch, but don't drop stitch off left-hand needle; now knit stitch again, this time through back of stitch) = total of 17 stitches. Knit 54 rows. Break off yarn and put stitches on holding needle or stitch holder. Work second leg the same way – but don't break off yarn. Knit next row, then knit stitches off holding needle from first leg – you now have a total of 34 stitches on needle for body.

BODY

Continue with black yarn and knit 74 rows. Break off yarn and switch to white yarn for middle part of body. Knit 168 rows (for a longer scarf, knit additional rows). Break off yarn and switch back to black yarn. Knit 22 rows with black yarn.

FRONT LEGS

Next row: *cast on 19 stitches for first front leg using open-knit cast-on (see illustration below), then knit row beginning with the stitches you just cast on and knit to end of row. Repeat from * on next row for second front leg = you now have a total of 72 stitches. Increase 1 stitch at the beginning of next 2 rows = total of 74 stitches. Knit 28 rows. *Knit next row to last 2 stitches, knit those 2 stitches together; repeat from * on next row. Bind off 19 stitches at the beginning of next 2 rows = 34 stitches remaining. *Knit row to last 2 stitches, knit those 2 stitches together; repeat from * on the next 3 rows. You've got 30 stitches remaining.

Open-Knit Cast-On

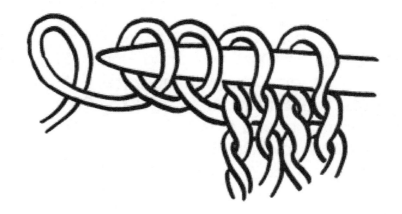

HEAD

Break off black yarn and switch to white yarn. Knit 2 rows. Next row: *knit 6 stitches, increase 1 stitch (increase by picking up yarn between stitches with left-hand needle; then knitting through back of loop over needle); repeat from * to end of row, ending row with knit 6 = you now have 34 stitches. Knit 3 rows. Next row: *knit 7 stitches, increase 1 stitch; repeat from * to end of row, ending row with knit 6. You have 38 stitches. Knit 33 rows. Next row: *knit 6 stitches, knit 2 stitches together; repeat from * to end of row, ending row with knit 6 = 34 stitches. Knit 5 rows. Next row: *knit 5 stitches, knit 2 together; repeat from * to end of row, ending row with knit 6 = 30 stitches. Knit 5 rows. Next row: *knit 4 stitches, knit 2 together; repeat from * to end of row 25 stitches. Knit 5 rows. Next row: *knit 3 stitches, knit 2 together; repeat from * to end of row = 20 stitches. Knit 3 rows. Next row: *knit 2 stitches, knit 2 together; repeat from * to end of row = 15 stitches. Knit 3 rows. Break off white yarn and switch to black yarn for nose: knit 6 rows. Next row: knit first stitch, then *knit 2 stitches together; repeat from * to end of row. Knit next row, then bind off in following row.

EARS

With black yarn pick up 10 stitches at edge of head as follows: right side facing you, for right ear (bear facing you) count 22 rows down from beginning of head (start counting at neck where you switched to white yarn) and pick up 1 stitch per 2 rows so ear ends up 2 rows in from beginning of head; for left year, start picking up 10 stitches 2 rows in from beginning of head.

Work ear as follows: knit 1 row. Next row: knit 1, *increase 1 stitch, knit 2; repeat from * ending row with increase 1 stitch and knit 1 = total of 15 stitches. Knit 8 rows. Next row: knit first stitch, *knit 2 together; repeat from * to end of row. Next row: *knit 2 together; repeat from * to end of row. Pull yarn through remaining stitches. Repeat for second year.

EYE PATCHES

With black yarn, cast on 8 stitches. Knit 1 row. Increase 1 stitch at the beginning of next row. Knit 2 rows. *Knit next row to last 2 stitches and knit those 2 stitches together. Knit 5 rows. Repeat from * until you have 5 stitches left, ending with 5 knit rows. Knit next row to last 2 stitches, knit those 2 stitches together. Bind off in next row. Repeat for second patch. Sew patches on face – flop second patch so both are symmetrical (check picture at beginning of pattern for positioning).

EYES?

My Panda Scarf is eye-less. If that bothers you, add little round felt eyes with a bead in the middle and sew on black patches. Better now?

Snake Scarf

Snakes and small boys pair up real easily. So if you know a little buddy that refuses to wear a scarf because they are too girlie, knit him a snake instead. Add a cool-looking cap in matching color and you've got him dressed for the cold. The pattern for the cap follows the Snake Scarf pattern.

Tip: If you can't find variegated yarn in your stash, use small amounts of different yarn colors. And if some of the yarn is ticker – all the better! – it will give the snake some ribs and ridges, or call it texture.

For a wider scarf, just add stitches to width and if you prefer a longer Snake, add rows to middle of body.

Size: About 58" long (147 cm) and about 6" wide (15 cm).

Yarn: Multi-colored sport weight yarn, 225 yards (206 m). Small amount of purple or red yarn for tongue. Sample is knit with Variegated Morehouse Merino 2-Ply.

Other Materials : Small piece of white or yellow felt for eyes; sewing thread to match felt color and black thread or yarn for stripes in eyes.

Needles : US 4 or 5 (3.5 mm or 3.75 mm; you'll also need a crochet hook size D or E (3.25 mm or 3.5 mm) for tongue.

Gauge: 20 stitches = 4" (10 cm) over stockinette stitch.

Start the Snake Scarf at the tip of the tail. Cast on 3 stitches and work 2 rows in stockinette stitch – knit on right side and purl on wrong side. Entire scarf is worked in stockinette stitch, so edges will curl slightly to give Snake Scarf a rounded look.

Row 3 : knit row to last stitch, increase 1 stitch (increase by picking up yarn between stitches with left-hand needle, then knitting through back of loop over needle), then knit last stitch.

Row 4 : purl.

Row 5: knit.

Row 6: purl.

Row 7: knit first stitch, increase 1 stitch, knit to end of row.

Row 8: purl.

Row 9: knit.

Row 10: purl.

Repeat Rows 3 through 10 until you have 29 to 35 stitches (depending on width you want). Now continue in stockinette stitch pattern until scarf measures 58" long (147 cm) , ending with a wrong side row. Work decrease rows as follows: knit first stitch, *knit 2 stitches together; repeat from * to end of row. Next row (wrong side): knit first stitch, *purl 2 stitches together; repeat from * to end of row, knit last stitch. Repeat decrease row one more time on right side. Purl row and bind off remaining stitches.

TONGUE

Use red or purple yarn double and crochet four or five chain stitches at tip of head of Snake, separate yarn and crochet 3 or 4 additional chain stitches with each piece of yarn for split tongue.

EYES

Cut out felt circle about ½" (a little over 1 cm) in diameter. With black sewing thread or yarn stitch a line through middle of circle (or you can use a sewing machine – cut felt into a 1-inch ribbon, then sew a line along the middle of strip with stitches as close together as possible, then cut out circles). Check picture of eyes in Critter Scarves. Sew eyes on head with sewing thread.

RIBBED CAP

For a matching Snake 'n Cap set, here is a pattern for a simple 1x1 rib hat.

Size: Child and adult.

Yarn: Multi-colored sport weight yarn to match Snake Scarf, 200 to 225 yards (183 m to 205 m).

Needles: Set of double-pointed US 3 or 4 (3.25 mm or 3.5 mm); you can knit cap with a 16" (40 cm) circular needle, then use double-pointed needles, same size or smaller, for the last few rounds when circumference of Cap gets too small for circular needle.

Gauge: 26 stitches = 4" (10 cm) over un-stretched rib pattern.

Cast on 92 (96) stitches using an elastic cast-on method, such as long-tail cast-on. Join for knitting in the round and start rib pattern worked as follows: *knit 1 stitch, purl 1 stitch; repeat from * to end of round. Work until Cap measures 9"to 10" (11") (23 cm to 25 cm, 28 cm for adult). If you are a using circular needle, switch to double-pointed needles for decrease rounds.

Decreases: knit first stitch, *knit 2 stitches together; repeat from * to last stitch. Knit last stitch together with first stitch of next round. Then work the next 2 rounds as follows: *knit 2 together; repeat from * to end of round. Pull yarn through remaining stitches.

CatWrap

This is the pattern where you pull out all stops! Raid your knitting repertoire for every trick you learned! Copy the cat you love or invent a feline fantasy. Use fluffy yarns, hairy mohair, felt and fake fur to embellish your CatWrap. And if you are skilled at spinning, use the real cat's hair (mixed with a little sheep wool for easier spinning) and you'll be able to knit a perfect duplicate of your pal with homespun yarn of authentic kitty fur. The choices here are dizzying. I'm including a picture a customer sent me of her very unique and absolutely fabulous CatWrap and you'll get an idea of how far you can go with this one! (See picture at the end of pattern.) For an extra-long CatWrap, simply add more stripes or rows to body.

In my pattern I alternate bulky with worsted weight yarn – each a different color – to give the Cat some life or texture. If you are using your home-spun yarn, you might have to double or triple it to get the right thickness for the bulky yarn. You can use sport weight with bulky, two colors, one color or multiple colors or a variegated yarn for a tabby cat. As the saying goes: there is more than one way to... well, let's call it *stitch* a cat! Be creative and have fun with this one! And take a look at that chef-d'oeuvre at the end of the pattern to get your creative juices flowing! It's a total Wow!

Size: About 40" long (102 cm) front leg to back leg; and about 5" wide (12.7 cm)

Yarn: If you follow the pattern you'll need 105 yards bulky (96 m) and 150 yards worsted weight (137 m). Sample is knit with Morehouse Merino Bulky in Natural BrownHeather and 3-Strand in Henna.

Needles: Double-pointed US 13 (9 mm); US 5 or 6 (3.75 mm or 4.25 mm). The CatWrap is knit back and forth on two needles, the

US 13 (9 mm) double-pointed needles are needed to knit separate parts (such as legs) then joining them as you knit along.

Other Materials : Small piece of yellow felt for eyes; sewing thread to match felt color and black thread or yarn for stripes in eyes.

Gauge: 12 stitches = 4" (10 cm) over garter stitch using bulky yarn (gauge on stripes with smaller needles and worsted weight yarn will be smaller and is not crucial).

FRONT LEGS

Start with the two front legs: with bulky yarn, using the larger needles (US 13, 9 mm), cast on 7 stitches and knit 7 rows. Next: *knit row to last 2 stitches, knit those 2 stitches together; repeat from * on next row = 5 stitches. Knit 28 rows. Break off yarn and leave stitches on needle. Make second leg the same way as first one. Break off yarn and leave stitches on needle.

HEAD

Start at the nose, with larger needle and bulky yarn, cast on 7 stitches and knit 2 rows.

Row 3: knit first stitch, increase 1 stitch (increase by picking up yarn between stitches with left-hand needle, then knitting through back of loop over needle), knit 2, increase 1 stitch, knit 1, increase 1, knit 2, increase 1, knit last stitch = 11 stitches.

Rows 4, 6, 8, 10, 12: knit.

Row 5: knit 1, increase 1, knit 4, increase 1, knit 1, increase 1, knit 4, increase 1, knit 1 = 15 stitches.

Row 7: knit 1, increase 1, knit 6, increase 1, knit 1, increase 1, knit 6, increase 1, knit 1 = 19 stitches.

Row 9: knit 1, increase 1, knit 8, increase 1, knit 1, increase 1, knit 8, increase 1, knit 1 = 23 stitches.

Row 11: knit 1, increase 1, knit 10, increase 1, knit 1, increase 1, knit 10, increase 1, knit 1 = 27 stitches.

Row 13: knit first stitch, *knit 2 stitches together; repeat from * 5 more times (for a total of 6 times knit-2-together), knit 1, *knit 2 stitches together; repeat from * 5 more times (again, for a total of 6 times), knit last stitch = 15 stitches.

Rows14-26: knit (13 rows).

EARS

Row 1: knit 2, cast on 10 stitches using e-loop cast-on (see illustration in Panda Scarf, pull yarn tight after each loop), knit 11, and cast on another 10 stitches, then knit the last 2 stitches = 35 stitches.

Rows 2, 4, 6, 8: knit.

Row 3: *knit 2 stitches together; repeat from * 3 more times (for a total of 4 times), knit 19 stitches, *knit 2 stitches together; repeat from * 3 more times (for a total of 4 times) = 27 stitches.

Row 5: knit 1, *knit 2 stitches together; repeat from * 2 more times, knit 13, *knit 2 stitches together; repeat from * 2 more times, knit last stitch = 21 stitches.

Row 7: knit 1, *knit 2 stitches together; repeat from * 2 more times, knit 7, *knit 2 stitches together; repeat from * 2 more times, knit last stitch = 15 stitches.

Rows 9 & 10: knit each row to last 2 stitches, knit those 2 stitches together = 13 stitches

Rows 11 & 12: increase 1 stitch at the beginning of each row (increase between first and second stitch) = 15 stitches.

BODY

Knit next row and attach the two front legs as follows: put needle with first leg parallel to needle you are working on – with the stitches for leg behind stitches you are working on. Now knit the first 5 stitches together with stitches on leg (how? knit the first stitch on needle closest to you together with the first stitch on needle in back – leg stitch – then knit second stitch on needle closest to you together with second stitch on needle in back, and so on); after first leg is attached, knit the next 5 stitches on body, then knit stitches on second leg together with the last 5 stitches on body. Knit next row. Now both legs are attached to body – dangling in back.

Start stripe pattern: using smaller needles and contrast yarn color (worsted weight), knit 2 rows. Switch back to bulky yarn and larger needles and knit 2 rows. Don't break off yarn after finishing the 2 rows – let yarn hang at side until you are ready to do the next 2 rows, then pull it up loosely at side and work 2 rows. Continue this way, alternating colors (and needle size) every 2 rows, until you have 25 stripes in contrast yarn color. Break off contrast yarn color. Finish body with 2 rows in bulky. Don't break off bulky yarn.

BACK LEGS & TAIL

Continue with bulky and larger needles. Knit the first 5 stitches, turn and knit the 5 stitches back to beginning of row. Continue working on these 5 stitches and knit 28 rows total for first back leg. Next: *knit first stitch, increase 1 stitch and knit the remaining stitches; repeat from * on next row = 7 stitches. Knit 7 more rows and bind off tightly.

Use the next 5 stitches on body for tail of cat: start *with contrast yarn color and smaller needles and knit 2 rows; switch to bulky yarn and larger needles and knit 2 rows; repeat from * until you have 15 stripes in contrast yarn color, ending with 2 rows in bulky. Break off bulky yarn and continue with contrast yarn color and smaller needles: knit 10 rows. Next row: knit the first and last 2 stitches together. Bind off remaining 3 stitches.

With the remaining 5 stitches on body, knit the second back leg the same way as the other back leg (using bulky yarn and larger needles).

EYES

Cut out 2 felt circles about ¾" (about 2 cm) in diameter. With black sewing thread or yarn stitch a line through middle of circle (or you can use a sewing machine – cut felt into a 1-inch ribbon, then sew a line along the middle of strip with stitches as close together as possible, then cut out circles). Check picture of eyes in Critter Scarves . Sew eyes on head with sewing thread.

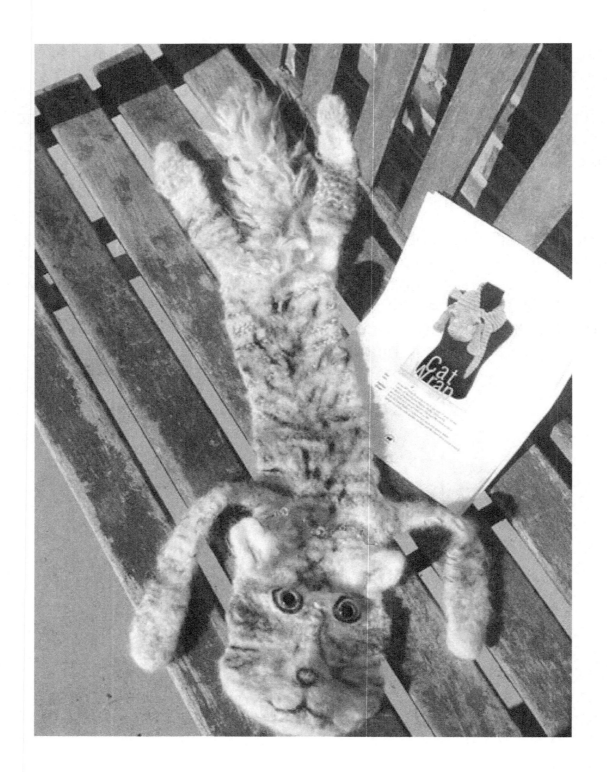

Owl Purse

Let's get the children involved! This pattern is written with young reader-knitters in mind. It's an easy project once they have mastered the basics of knitting. You might want to look over their shoulder every once in a while to make sure they are on the right track and knitting an Owl Purse and not just a pot holder. The instructions include a few additional pointers and plenty of pictures to keep things clicking smoothly for young knitters.

Tip: Want to make a really awesome-looking Owl Purse? How about adding fringe along the bottom and the sides, then brushing the fringe with a hair brush to make it look like wooly feathers or feathery wool.

Size: About 6½" wide (16.5 cm) and 6" high (15 cm).

Yarn: Strong and tightly spun sport weight yarn, 225 yards (206 m) in brown or other owl color; small amount of yellow yarn for beak. Sample is knit with Morehouse Merino Gator Yarn.

Needles: US 4 or 5 (3.5 mm or 3.75 mm).

Other Materials : Small pieces of dark green (or black) and yellow felt for eyes; sewing thread to match felt colors.

Notions: A few pins for sewing strap together.

Gauge: 20 stitches = 4" (10 cm) over garter stitch.

ABOUT THE PATTERN

It's called garter stitch pattern when every row is a knit row. There is no right or wrong side, both sides look alike.

BEGINNING OF PURSE

Cast on 27 stitches and knit 2 rows. On the next row, we'll add small holes to thread braided string through later. Here is how it is done: knit 3 stitches, then pick up the strand of yarn between the stitch you just knit and the next stitch. Pick it up with the needle in your left hand (see pictures), then knit the loop over the needle as if it were a regular stitch. This will create a small hole below that loop stitch – and that's what we want for threading the string through.

Repeat the entire sequence again and again along the whole row: knit 3 stitches, then pick up the yarn between stitches and knit the loop and so on, until you get to the last 3 stitches. Knit the last 3 stitches. Now you'll have35 stitches on the needle (all the loop stitches are now added to your stitch count). Knit until the Purse measures 10½" (27 cm).

EARS & FOLD-OVER FLAP WITH BEAK

Next we are going to knit the part with the ears. We'll add new stitches at the sides so ears will stick out on both the left and the right side. Here is how: on the next row, knit the first stitch, then pick up the yarn between the first and the second stitch with the needle in your left hand, then knit the loop like an ordinary stitch (just like before). Then knit stitches to end of row. Repeat this same row (pick up a new stitch between the first and second stitch on every row) until you have 43 stitches on the needle. Then knit the next 2 rows without adding new stitches. This is the tip of the ears. Now we'll start to decrease stitches so face will get narrower with each row, all the way to the beak. Here is how: knit stitches on the needle to the last 2 stitches and knit those 2 stitches together (knit them as if they were one stitch). Repeat this row over and over again until you have 5 stitches left for beak. Check the picture to see what the Owl Purse now looks like.

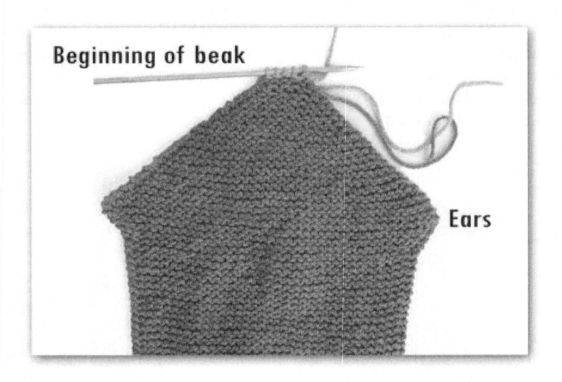

Beginning of beak

Ears

BEAK

Break off the brown yarn (leave a short tail to darn in later) and switch to the yellow yarn for the beak. Knit the brown stitches with the yellow yarn. Then knit 8 rows. And on the next row knit 3 stitches, then knit the last 2 stitches together. And on next row knit 2 stitches and knit the last 2 stitches together. Bind off the last 3 stitches in the following row. Darn in yarn ends at the beak.

STRAP

Cast on 10 stitches and knit until strap measures 26" (66 cm). Bind off. Roll strap into a sausage-like roll and keep it together with pins, then sew it together. Keep 1" open at both ends for sewing the straps to the back of the Purse. Check the picture on the left side.

FINISHING
Fold the beginning of the Purse up to where the ears begin. Sew the sides together. Then turn Owl Purse inside out. Sew the tips of each ear together so they'll look like pointy cones. Sew the straps on the back of the Bag where the ears start. Check the picture on the right side.

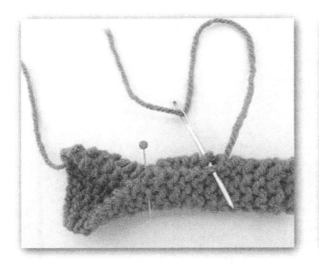 

Next you'll need to braid 2 strings each 10" long (25 cm). Cut 6 pieces of yarn each 20" long (50 cm) and use 3 pieces per string. Attach each piece to one side of the Purse on the front where the ears begin. Then thread the braids through the holes that you knit in the third row at the beginning of the Purse. The braids should meet in the middle of the Purse so they can be tied together. Look at the picture at the end of the pattern and you'll see what it will look like.

Then cut out felt eyes: 2 yellow eyes 1 inch (2.5 cm) big and 2 dark eyes to fit inside yellow ones. Sew the small dark circle on the big yellow circle (use regular sewing thread and sew with tiny stitches). Then sew yellow eyes on the Purse. Make sure they are in the right position so they peek out from under the flap when you close down the flap. This is what the finished Owl Purse looks like with the flap open.

Wasn't that easy and fun?

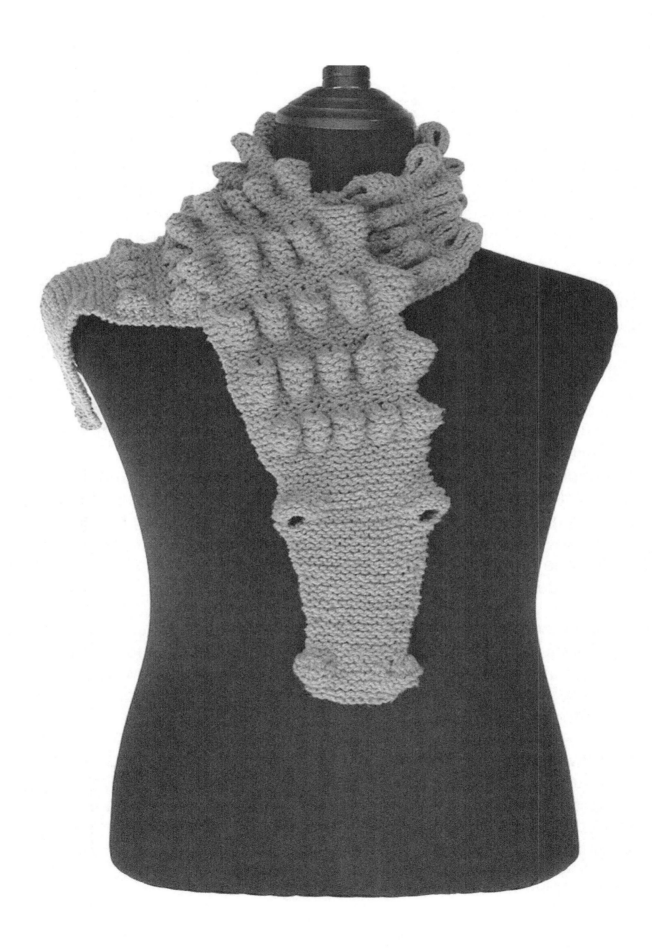

Alligator Scarf

This Gator Pattern has been all over the world: from Japan to Greece, from Iceland to Brazil, from the UK to South Korea and across Europe to Israel. Knitters form all around the world have had fun making Alligator Scarves. It's the most popular Morehouse Farm Critter – by far! Little did I realize how well-liked this scarf would be when I designed it. I was, quite frankly, a little skeptical: am I going too far with these Critter Knits? Will anybody really enjoy wrapping a bumpy Alligator Scarf around their neck? I soon found out that the answer is a thunderous YES! There seem to be thousands of Gator Fans out there, and I'm not just talking about the ones in Florida!

The Gator was also the turning point in my pattern writing career: after its popularity became clear, I re-wrote the pattern line for line and without knitting abbreviations. It made our life here at Morehouse Farm a lot easier (fewer queries and emails) and it helped thousands of knitters to a successful Gator Scarf. Some may call this dumbing down a pattern, I call it accommodating knitters of all skill levels. While it definitely added to the length of the pattern it also made reading it and knitting from it a more pleasurable experience.

Here are some observations from fans. One knitter wrote: "As soon as I finished the head, I started to talk to my Gator…" and another knitter shared this story: "The only time my husband showed the slightest interest in my knitting was while knitting the Gator…!"(must be a Florida Gator fan!)

So now you can join the fan club! I suggest that you knit the pattern as written except for length: you can add or delete "bumps" to shorten or lengthen the scarf (in *Body, Main Part*). You can also stripe the Gator, of course, and add eyes (I have eye sockets, not actual eyes, and some knitters prefer to add eyes).

Enjoy and don't forget to say "Hello" to your Gator!

Size: About 56" long (142 cm) and 6" wide (15 cm).

Yarn: 450 yards (412 m) of tightly spun sport weight yarn. The yarn needs to have a firm twist, so the bumps on the Gator don't go limp after washing. Sample is knit with 2 skeins of Morehouse Merino Gator Yarn, a sport weight yarn with a tight twist that gets softer with each washing.

Needles : US 5 or 6 (3.75 mm or 4.25 mm).

Gauge: 20 stitches = 4" (10 cm) over garter stitch.

Start the Alligator Scarf at the tip of the nose. Cast on 9 stitches. Knit 4 rows.

NOSTRILS

Row 1: knit 1, increase 1 stitch (increase by picking up yarn between stitches with left-hand needle, then knitting through back of loop over needle), knit 1, increase 1, knit 5, increase 1, knit 1, increase 1, knit last stitch = 13 stitches.

Rows 2, 4, 6 & 8: knit.

Row 3: knit 1, increase 1, knit 3, increase 1, knit 5, increase 1, knit 3, increase 1, knit last stitch = 17 stitches.

Row 5: knit 1, increase 1, knit 5, increase 1, knit 5, increase 1, knit 5, increase 1, knit last stitch = 21 stitches.

Row 7: knit 1, increase 1, knit 7, increase 1, knit 5, increase 1, knit 7, increase 1, knit 1 = 25 stitches.

Row 9: knit 1, *knit 3 together; repeat from * 2 more times, knit 5, *knit 3 together; repeat from * 2 more times, knit last stitch = 13 stitches.

Row 10: knit 1, knit 2 together, knit 7, knit 2 together, knit 1 = 11 stitches.

PLEASE NOTE: From here on, all even rows are knit.

HEAD

Rows 1-12: knit (12 rows).

Row 13: knit and increase 1 stitch each at the beginning and end of row (increase between first and second and between next-to-last and last stitches) = 13 stitches.

Rows 14-24: knit (11 rows).

Row 25: knit and increase 1 stitch each at the beginning and end of row (same as above) = 15 stitches.

Rows 26-34: knit (9 rows).

Row 35: knit and increase 1 stitch each at beginning and end of row (same as above) = 17 stitches.

Rows 36-38: knit (3 rows).

EYES

Row 1: knit 2, cast on 9 stitches (use e-loop cast-on method, see illustration in Panda Scarf), knit 13, cast on 9 stitches, knit 2 = 35 stitches.

Row 3: knit 1, knit 2 together, knit 7, knit 2 together, knit 11, knit 2 together, knit 7, knit 2 together, knit 1 = 31 stitches.

Row 5: knit 1, knit 2 together, knit 5, knit 2 together, knit 11, knit 2 together, knit 5, knit 2 together, knit 1 = 27 stitches.

Row 7: knit 1, knit 2 together, knit 3, knit 2 together, knit 11, knit 2 together, knit 3, knit 2 together, knit 1 = 23 stitches.

Row 9: knit 1, knit 2 together, knit 1, knit 2 together, knit 11, knit 2 together, knit 1, knit 2 together, knit 1 = 19 stitches.

Row 11: knit 2, knit 2 together, knit 11, knit 2 together, knit 2 = 17 stitches.

Rows 12-16: knit (5 rows).

Row 17: knit and increase 1 stitch each at the beginning and end of row (same as Row 13 in *Alligator Head*) = 19 stitches.

Rows 18-20: knit (3 rows).

BODY, FIRST PART

Row 1: knit 3, increase 1, knit 1, increase 1, *knit 2, increase 1, knit 1, increase 1; repeat from * to last 3 stitches, knit 3 = 29 stitches.

Row 3: knit 3, increase 1, knit 3, increase 1, *knit 2, increase 1, knit 3, increase 1; repeat from * to last 3 stitches, knit 3 = 39 stitches.

Row 5: knit 3, increase 1, knit 5, increase 1, *knit 2, increase 1, knit 5, increase 1; repeat from * to last 3 stitches, knit 3 = 49 stitches.

Row 7: knit 3, increase 1, knit 7, increase 1, *knit 2, increase 1, knit 7, increase 1; repeat from * to last 3 stitches, knit 3 = 59 stitches.

Row 9: knit 3, *bind off 8 stitches tightly (count stitches as you are binding them off, not as you are knitting them), knit 3 (includes stitch on needle from last bind-off); repeat from * to last 4 stitches, knit 4 = 19 stitches. This is what stitches look like on needle: 3 stitches, then a hole where you bind off 8, 3 stitches again, another hole from bind-off, etc., ending with 4 stitches.

Row 10: knit row and pull yarn tight between bind-off stitches.

Rows 11-14: knit (4 rows).

BODY, SECOND PART

Row 15: knit 3, increase 1, *knit 1, increase 1; rep from * to last 3 stitches, knit 3 = 33 stitches.

Row 17: knit 3, *increase 1, knit 3; repeat from * to end of row = 43 stitches.

Row 19: knit 3, *increase 1, knit 5, increase 1, knit 3; repeat from * to end of row = 53 stitches.

Row 21: knit 3, *increase 1, knit 7, increase 1, knit 3; repeat from * to end of row = 63 stitches.

Row 23: knit 3, *increase 1, knit 9, increase 1, knit 3; repeat from * to end of row = 73 stitches.

Row 25: knit 3, *bind off 10 stitches tightly (count stitches as you are binding them off, not as you are knitting them), knit 4 (includes stitch on needle from last bind-off); repeat from * to end of row = 23 stitches.

Row 26: knit row and pull yarn tight between bind-off stitches.

Rows 27-30: knit (4 rows).

BODY, MAIN PART

Row 31: knit 3, *increase 1, knit 1, increase 1, knit 3; repeat from * to end of row = 33 stitches.

Row 33: knit 3, *increase 1, knit 3; repeat from * to end of row = 43 stitches.

Row 35: knit 3, *increase 1, knit 5, increase 1, knit 3; repeat from * to end of row = 53 stitches.

Row 37: knit 3, *increase 1, knit 7, increase 1, knit 3; repeat from * to end of row = 63 stitches.

Row 39: knit 3, *increase 1, knit 9, increase 1, knit 3; repeat from * to end of row = 73 stitches.

Row 41: knit 3, *bind off 10 stitches tightly, knit 4 (includes stitch on needle from last bind-off); repeat from * to end of row = 23 stitches.

Row 42: knit row and pull yarn tight between bind-off stitches.

Rows 43-46: knit (4 rows).

Repeat rows 31 to 46 twelve times (total body length: 16 rows x 12 = 192 rows + rows 1 through 30 = total of 222).

TAIL

Row 1: knit 3, *increase 1, knit 1, increase 1, knit 1, knit 2 together; repeat from * to last 4 stitches, end row with increase 1, knit 1, increase 1, knit 3 = 29 stitches.

Row 3: knit 3, increase 1, knit 3, increase 1, *knit 2, increase 1, knit 3, increase 1; repeat from * to last 3 stitches, knit 3 = 39 stitches.

Row 5: knit 3, increase 1, knit 5, increase 1, *knit 2, increase 1, knit 5, increase 1; repeat from * to last 3 stitches, knit 3 = 49 stitches.

Row 7: knit 3, increase 1, knit 7, increase 1, *knit 2, increase 1, knit 7, increase 1; repeat from * to last 3 stitches, knit 3 = 59 stitches.

Row 9: knit 3, *bind off 8 stitches tightly, knit 3 (includes stitch on needle from last bind-off); repeat from * to last stitch, knit 1 = 19 stitches.

Row 10: knit row and pull yarn tight between bind-off stitches.

Rows 11-14: knit (4 rows).

Row 15: knit 3, increase 1, knit 1, increase 1, *knit 2 together, increase 1, knit 1, increase 1; repeat from * to last 3 stitches, knit 3 = 25 stitches.

Row 17: knit 3, increase 1, knit 3, increase 1, *knit 1, increase 1, knit 3, increase 1; repeat from * to last 3 stitches, knit 3 = 35 stitches.

Row 19: knit 3, increase 1, knit 5, increase 1, *knit 1, increase 1, knit 5, increase 1; repeat from * to last 3 stitches, knit 3 = 45 stitches.

Row 21: knit 3, *bind off 6 stitches tightly, knit 2 (includes stitch on needle from last bind-off); repeat from * to last 2 stitches, knit 2 = 15 stitches.

Rows 22-36: knit (15 rows).

Row 37: knit first 2 stitches together, knit row to last 2 stitches, knit those 2 stitches together = 13 stitches.

Rows 38-52: knit (15 rows).

Row 53: repeat row 37 = 11 stitches.

Rows 54-66: knit (13 rows).

Row 67: repeat row 37 = 9 stitches.

Rows 68-78: knit (11 rows).

Row 79: repeat row 37 = 7 stitches.

Rows 80-88: knit (9 rows).

Row 89: repeat row 37 = 5 stitches.

Rows 90-96: knit (7 rows).

Row 97: repeat row 37 = 3 stitches.

Bind off the last 3 stitches. And you are done!

Baby Alligator Scarf

This is the little cousin to the Big Gator. Same basic concept – but everything is scaled down on this little guy: its bumps, its width and length. With its pint-sized proportions, it is meant for wee folks.

Size: About 36" (91 cm) long and 4½" (11.5 cm) wide.

Yarn: 225 yards (206 m) of tightly spun sport weight yarn. The yarn needs to have a firm twist, so the bumps on the Gator don't go limp after washing.

Needles : US 5 or 6 (3.75 mm or 4.25 mm).

Gauge: 20 stitches = 4"(10 cm) over garter stitch.

Start the Baby Alligator Scarf at the tip of the nose. Cast on 8 stitches. Knit 4 rows.

ALLIGATOR NOSTRILS

Row 1: knit 1, increase 1 (increase by picking up yarn between stitches with left-hand needle, then knitting through back of loop over needle), knit 1, increase 1, knit 4, increase 1, knit 1, increase 1, knit last stitch = 12 stitches.

Rows 2, 4, 6 & 8: knit.

Row 3: knit 1, increase 1, knit 3, increase 1, knit 4, increase 1, knit 3, increase 1, knit last stitch = 16 stitches.

Row 5: knit 1, increase 1, knit 5, increase 1, knit 4, increase 1, knit 5, increase 1, knit last stitch = 20 stitches.

Row 7: knit 1, increase 1, knit 7, increase 1, knit 4, increase 1, knit 7, increase 1, knit 1 = 24 stitches.

Row 9: knit 1, *knit 3 together; repeat from * 2 more times, knit 4, *knit 3 together; repeat from * 2 more times, knit last stitch = 12 stitches.

Row 10: Knit 1, knit 2 together, knit 6, knit 2 together, knit 1 = 10 stitches.

PLEASE NOTE: From here on, all even rows are knit.

HEAD

Rows 1-12: knit (12 rows.

Row 13: knit and increase 1 stitch each at beginning and end of row (increase between first & second and between next-to-last & last stitches) = 12 stitches.

Rows 14-24: knit (11 rows).

Row 25: knit and increase 1 stitch each at beginning and end of row (same as above) = 14 stitches.

Rows 26-28: knit (3 rows).

Row 29: knit and increase 1 stitch each at beginning and end of row (same as above) = 16 stitches.

Row 30: knit (1 row).

EYES

Row 1: knit 2, cast on 8 stitches (use e-loop cast-on method, see illustration in Panda Scarf), knit 12, cast on 8 stitches, knit 2 = 32 stitches.

Row 3: knit 1, knit 2 together, knit 6, knit 2 together, knit 10, knit 2 together, knit 6, knit 2 together, knit 1 = 28 stitches.

Row 5: knit 1, knit 2 together, knit 4, knit 2 together, knit 10, knit 2 together, knit 4, knit 2 together, knit 1 = 24 stitches.

Row 7: knit 1, knit 2 together, knit 2, knit 2 together, knit 10, knit 2 together, knit 2, knit 2 together, knit 1 = 20 stitches.

Row 9: knit 1, *knit 2 together; repeat from *, knit 10, *knit 2 together; repeat from *, knit 1 = 16 stitches.

Row 11: knit 2, knit 2 together, knit 8, knit 2 together, knit 2=14 stitches.

Rows 12-14: knit (3 rows).

Row 15: knit and increase 1 stitch each at beginning and end of row (same as Row 13 in *Alligator Head*) = 16 stitches.

Rows 16-18: knit (3 rows).

BODY, FIRST PART

Row 1: knit 3, increase 1, knit 1, increase 1, *knit 2, increase 1, knit 1, increase 1; repeat from * to last 3 stitches, knit 3 = 24 stitches.

Row 3: knit 3, increase 1, knit 3, increase 1, *knit 2, increase 1, knit 3, increase 1; repeat from * to last 3 stitches, knit 3 = 32 stitches.

Row 5: knit 3, increase 1, knit 5, increase 1, *knit 2, increase 1, knit 5, increase 1; repeat from * to last 3 stitches, knit 3 = 40 stitches.

Row 7: knit 3, *bind off 6 stitches tightly (count stitches as you are binding them off, not as you are knitting them), knit 3 (includes stitch on needle from last bind-off); repeat from * to last stitch, knit 1 = 16 stitches. This is what it will look like on needle: 3 stitches, then a hole where you bind off 6, 3 stitches again, another hole from bind-off, etc., ending with 4 stitches.

Row 8: knit row and pull yarn tight between bind-off stitches.

Rows 9-12: knit (4 rows).

BODY, SECOND PART

Row 13: knit 3, increase 1, *knit 1, increase 1; repeat from * to last 3 stitches, knit 3 = 27 stitches.

Row 15: knit 3, *increase 1, knit 3; repeat from * to end of row = 35 stitches.

Row 17: knit 3, *increase 1, knit 5, increase 1, knit 3; repeat from * to end of row = 43 stitches.

Row 19: knit 3, *bind off 6 stitches tightly, knit 4 (includes stitch on needle from last bind-off); repeat from * to end of row = 19 stitches (this row is similar to Row 7 in *Body, First Part*)

Row 20: knit row, tighten yarn between bind-off stitches.

Rows 21-24: knit (4 rows).

BODY, MAIN PART

Row 25: knit 3, *increase 1, knit 1, increase 1, knit 3; repeat from * to end of row = 27 stitches.

Rows 27-36: Repeat Rows 15-24 from *Body, Second Part*.

Repeat rows 25 to 36 fifteen times (total body length: 12 rows x 15 = 180 rows + rows 1 through 24 = total of

204 rows).

TAIL

Row 1: knit 3, *increase 1, knit 1, increase 1, knit 1, knit 2 together; repeat from * to last 4 stitches, end row with increase 1, knit 1, increase 1, knit 3 = 24 stitches.

Row 3: knit 3, increase 1, knit 3, increase 1, *knit 2, increase 1, knit 3, increase 1; repeat from * to last 3 stitches, knit 3 = 32 stitches.

Row 5: knit 3, increase 1, knit 5, increase 1, *knit 2, increase 1, knit 5, increase 1; repeat from * to last 3 stitches, knit 3 = 40 stitches.

Row 7: knit 3, *bind off 6 stitches tightly, knit 3 (includes stitch on needle from last bind-off); repeat from * to last stitch, knit 1 = 16 stitches.

Row 8: knit row, tighten yarn between bind-off stitches.

Rows 9-12: knit (4 rows).

Row 13: knit 3, increase 1, knit 1, increase 1, *knit 2 together, increase 1, knit 1, increase 1; repeat from * to last 3 stitches, knit 3 = 21 stitches.

Row 15: knit 3, increase 1, knit 3, increase 1, *knit 1, increase 1, knit 3, increase 1; repeat from * to last 3 stitches, knit 3 = 29 stitches.

Row 17: knit 3, *bind off 4 stitches tightly, knit 2 (includes stitch on needle from last bind-off); repeat from * to last 2 stitches, knit 2 = 13 stitches.

Row 18-32: knit (15 rows).

Row 33: knit first 2 stitches together, knit row to last 2 stitches, knit those 2 stitches together = 11 stitches.

Tip of Tail: knit 13 rows, then repeat row 33 = 9 stitches; knit 11 rows, then repeat row 33 = 7 stitches; knit 9 rows, then repeat row 33 = 5 stitches; knit 7 rows, then repeat row 33 = 3 stitches; knit 1 row, then bind off last 3 stitches.

Gator Mittens

For a true Gator fan, this is a must-have pair of mittens. Unfortunately, big Gator fans are left out in the cold – these mittens are sized for children's hands. I can't quite convince myself that Gator Mittens look cool (never mind cute) on larger hands.

Children Sizes: Small, medium and large; mitten length (not including cuff and claw tips) 3½", 4" and 4½" (9 cm, 10 cm and 11.5 cm); or length to fit child's hand.

Yarn: About 220 yards (200 m) of sport weight yarn. Sample pair is knit with Morehouse Merino Gator Yarn.

Needles : Set of double-pointed US 4 or 5 (3.5 mm or 3.75 mm) or size to obtain gauge.

Notions : Small stitch holder or paper clip.

Gauge: 5.5 stitches = 1" (2.5 cm) over stockinette stitch.

CUFF

Cast on 27 (31/35) stitches. Join for knitting in the round and work cuff as follows: *purl 1 round, knit 1 round; repeat from * for a total of 16 (18/20) rounds.

THUMB GUSSET

Work next round as follows: *knit 1 stitch, increase 1 stitch (increase by picking up yarn between stitches with left-hand needle, then knitting through back of loop over needle); repeat from * 2 more times (you'll have 6 stitches on right-hand needle). Continue round as follows: *knit 5 (6/7) stitches, increase 1 stitch; repeat from * 2 more times; knit the next 5 (6/7) stitches; and end round with *knit 1 stitch, increase 1 stitch; repeat from * 2 more times; knit last stitch – total of 36 (40/44) stitches. Knit 12 (14/16) rounds. Next, knit round to last 4 stitches, put the last 4 stitches and first 4 stitches (from next round) on a stitch holder or paper clip. You now have 28 (32/36) stitches on needles. Pull yarn tight between last stitch and first stitch on needle to avoid gap where you put stitches on holder. Knit 20 (22/24) rounds or length to cover child's fingers.

CLAWS

Put stitches on 2 needles – 14 (16/18) stitches on each needle. Knitting the claws will feel a little awkward at first because the needles are parallel to each other. For first claw, put the first 3 (4/5) stitches on a separate needle and the last 4 stitches on another needle. With these 7 (8/9) stitches you'll knit the first claw. Knit the 3 (4/5) stitches on first needle; then knit the 4 stitches on last needle (pull yarn tight between needles). That's your first round for claw. Work next round as follows: *knit 1, knit 2 together; repeat from *, knit remaining stitch(es) – if any – at end of round. Knit 1 round. Repeat decrease round (knit 1, knit 2 together). Then pull yarn through remaining stitches. Second claw: put the next 4 stitches on first needle and the last 3 (4/5) stitches on the other needle and knit claw the same way as the first one. Work third claw the same way as the first one; and the fourth claw the same way as the second one.

THUMB

Put stitches from holding needle on two needles. Pick up 3 (3/4) stitches between first and last stitch – total of 11(11/12) stitches for thumb. Knit 10 (11/12) rounds. Work next round as follows: *knit 1, knit 2 together; repeat from * to end of round, knit remaining stitch(es) – if any – at end of round. Knit 1 round. Repeat decrease round (knit 1, knit 2 together). Then pull yarn through remaining stitches.

Loon Backpack

Among fashionable designer backpacks, this one's a stand-out! It's super charming and the monochromatic colors make it one classy way to tote your stuff around.

I would recommend that you knit the pattern as written, expect perhaps with color changes (pink loon anyone?). Choose a firm yarn (tightly spun) so Backpack can withstand some rough handling and being dragged around. And make sure that the yarn you use will felt. If in doubt, make a swatch using the **Body Pattern** (see below), then put it through the washing machine using hot water. There should be little or no shrinkage since you'll be knitting the Loon tight and the pattern itself adds to the firmness and stability.

Size: About 12" x 12" (30.5 cm x 30.5 cm).

Yarn: Sport weight yarn with a tight twist, 450 yards (411 m) in black, 225 yards (206 m) in white; small amount of charcoal or dark grey yarn color for beak and feet. Sample is knit with 3 skeins of Morehouse Merino Gator Yarn, a sport weight yarn with a tight twist.

Other Materials : 2 clear plastic eyes, ¾" in diameter (18 mm).

Needles : Set of double-pointed US 4 or 5 (3.5 mm or 3.75 mm); 24" (60 cm) circular needle US 4 or 5 (3.5 mm or 3.75 mm).

Notion : Stitch marker.

Gauge: 24 stitches = 4" (10 cm) over pattern for body of Loon (Backpack should be knit tight, so there will be very little shrinkage from felting).

Loon Backpack is knit from the bottom up towards the head. Bottom is flat with yarn double and is knit working back and forth. Then stitches are picked up along three sides of bottom and body of Loon will be worked in the round. Bottom, border at top, head, feet and straps are all worked using yarn double – working with two strands of yarn simultaneously. If you are knitting with skeins of yarn, make sure you wind them into two separate balls for each color..

BOTTOM

With black yarn used double (knit from two balls of yarn) and using two needles form the set of double-pointed needles, cast on 44 stitches. Knit 30 rows. Continue with yarn single (break off one of the strands of yarn). Work next row as follows: *knit 3 stitches, knit next stitch twice (knit stitch, but don't drop stitch off left-hand needle; knit into same stitch again, but this time through the back of the stitch). Repeat from * to end of row = 55 stitches total. Start with a new needle and pick up stitches at side of bottom, along rows you just knit: pick up 1 stitch per 2 rows, and pick up 1 additional stitch at each corner (beginning and end of side) = 17 stitches. Start a new needle and pick up stitches along cast-on edge as follows: pick up 1 stitch per stitch and every 4th stitch, pick up 1 extra stitch = 55 stitches total. Start a new needle again and pick up stitches along side same as before = 17 stitches. You now have a total of 144 stitches. From now on you'll be knitting in the round for body of Loon. Mark beginning of round with a stitch marker or a piece of different-colored yarn.

BODY

For the first 15 or so rounds, you'll have to use the double-pointed needles. Once Backpack begins to get rounder, you'll be able to switch to circular needle. For body of Backpack, you'll be switching yarn color every 2 rounds.

Body Pattern

Round 1: *knit 1 stitch, slip 1 stitch (slip stitch as if to purl stitch, with yarn in back); repeat from * to end of round.

Round 2: knit.

Start with black yarn color and work these 2 rounds in Body Pattern; switch to white yarn color and repeat the 2 rounds, then repeat the 2 rounds with black yarn color again, etc. Don't break off yarn after finishing 2 rounds and switching to new color, leave yarn hanging on inside of Backpack and bring up new yarn color behind color you just finished with – new color over old color – to avoid creating a hole where you switch yarn colors. Work in pattern, switching yarn color every 2 rounds, until you have 16 stripes in white. Switch to black and work 4 rounds in pattern. Next, work 2 rounds in white, followed by 6 rounds in black. Next, work 2 rounds in white again, followed by 8 rounds in black (maintaining Body Pattern). Backpack should measure about 9" (not including bottom). If you are short, add more rounds in black.

BORDER
Entire border is worked with yarn double and switching yarn color every 2 rounds. Start with white color and use yarn double. Knit next round as follows: knit 3 stitches, knit 2 stitches together; repeat from * to end of round, ending round with knit 4 = 116 stitches remaining. Purl next round.

Border Pattern

Round 1: knit.

Round 2: purl.

Work next 2 rounds in Border Pattern in black, then 2 rounds in white, and 2 more rounds in black color. Work next round (in white) as follows (this will be the eyelet round for threading tie string through): knit 3 stitches, *yarn over, knit 2 stitches together, knit 10 stitches; repeat from * a total of 6 times (you'll have worked a total of 75 stitches). Continue with: yarn over, knit 2 stitches together, then knit 6 stitches; knit 2 stitches together, yarn over; *knit 10 stitches, yarn over, knit 2 together; repeat from * one more time; end round with knit 7 stitches. Purl next round (purl yarn-overs as regular stitches).

Switch to black yarn color and work 2 rounds in Border Pattern followed by 2 more rounds in white. Switch to black yarn and knit round, then purl next round and bind off as follows: purl 31 stitches, then purl and bind off remaining stitches. Start next round: knit and bind off the first 13 stitches = 18 stitches remaining. These 18 stitches are for head.

HEAD

Entire head is knit with black yarn used double. You'll be knitting back and forth for head. Next 2 rows: knit row to last 2 stitches, knit those 2 stitches together = 16 stitches. Then knit 10 rows. Next 2 rows: knit row to last 2 stitches, knit those 2 stitches together = 14 stitches. Knit 8 rows. *Increase at the beginning of next 2 rows (work increases by knitting first stitch twice – same as on bottom of Backpack). Knit 2 rows. Repeat from * until you have 20 stitches. Knit 8 rows. Knit next row as follows: knit 3 stitches, yarn over needle, knit the next 2 stitches together; knit row to last 5 stitches; knit 2 together, yarn over and knit remaining 3 stitches (this row creates 2 eyelets for inserting eyes). Knit next row. *Next 2 rows: knit row to last 2 stitches, knit those 2 stitches together. Knit 2 rows. Repeat from * until you have 12 stitches left, ending with knit 2 rows. *Knit row to last 2 stitches, knit those 2 stitches together; repeat from * until you have 6 stitches left. Break off black yarn. Use charcoal yarn color for beak, use yarn double. Work 6 rows in stockinette stitch pattern (knit on right side, purl on wrong side). Next row: knit row to last 2 stitches, knit those 2 stitches together. Purl next row to last 2 stitches and purl those 2 stitches together. Work 6 more rows in stockinette stitch pattern. Pull yarn through stitches.

FEET

Use charcoal yarn double. Feet are attached to cast-on row on. (Confused which row is the cast-on row? The side with the head will be the back side and the feet are attached to the front side of the bottom part of the Backpack.) Count 12 stitches from beginning of cast-on row and pick up 5 stitches beginning with 13th cast-on stitch. Pick up 1 stitch per cast-on stitch. Knit 1 row. Increase at beg of next 2 rows = 7 stitches. Knit next row. Work next row as follows: knit 1, increase 1 (increase by picking up yarn between stitches with left-hand needle and knitting through back of loop over needle), knit 5, increase 1, knit last stitch = 9 stitches. Knit next row. Next row: knit 2, increase 1, knit 5, increase 1, knit 2 = 11 stitches. Knit next row. Next row: knit 3, increase 1, knit 5, increase 1, knit 3 = 13 stitches. Knit next row. Next row: knit 4, increase 1, knit 5, increase 1, knit 4 = 15 stitches. Knit next row. Next row: knit 5, increase 1, knit 5, increase 1, knit 5 = 17 stitches. Knit next row. Next row: knit first stitch, cast on 1 (using open-knit cast-on), bind off cast-on stitch and 5 additional stitches; knit next stitch and cast on 1 stitch; then bind off 6 stitches (including the new cast-on stitch); knit next stitch and cast on 1 stitch; then bind off all remaining stitches. The cast-on stitches create little "claws" at each tip of webbed foot. For second foot count 10 stitches between feet and pick up 5 stitches, then work same as first foot.

STRAPS

Straps are knit with yarn double. With black yarn color double, cast on 5 stitches and knit 200 rows. Next: bind off 4 stitches. Continue along side of strap and pick up stitches as follows: pick up 1 stitch per 2 rows. As you are picking up stitches, bind them off. This additional row along the edge of the strap reinforces the strap and prevents it from stretching out. When you reach the bottom of the strap, break off yarn and start along other edge of strap and pick up stitches and bind them off. Knit second strap. Sew straps to backpack in last 4 or 5 rounds of border at top – right behind head (there should be about 2" [5 cm] space between straps). Make sure you don't cover eyelet holes. Don't sew other end of strap to

Backpack yet – felt Backpack first, then sew them to bottom of Backpack at proper length.

TIE
Crochet or braid cord, using black color double and white color single (3 strands of yarn total), 40" long (102 cm). Thread tie through eyelet holes beginning in middle of front.

FINISHING
Darn in ends. Then felt Backpack in washing machine (hot water wash, hot water rinse, add some mild soap). Air dry (insert 2 regular-sized rolls of paper towels into Backpack for drying – this will prevent creases from forming and will give the Loon a nice round shape). When completely dry, add eyes.

MORE ABOUT THOSE EYES
If you are having trouble locating plastic eyes at your local crafts store, you can order them from our website:
http://www.morehousefarm.com/KnittingKits/Accessories/CritterEyes/
.

Order the18 mm clear plastic ones. A word of caution about them: the eyes come with a shank and you clip a washer onto shank on the inside. Once that washer is clipped on, it cannot be removed – so make sure the eyes are in the exact position that you want them to be in, before you add the washer!

Lobster Mittens

Probably the most unusual pair you'll ever knit: Lobster Claw Mitts with moveable claws. After the pair was featured in Vogue Knitting, we got lots of requests for an adult version. So I knit a pair of Lobster Mittens to fit an adult-sized hand. Guess what? Instead of looking like lobster claws, they ended up resembling a pair of boxing gloves! So I gave up, sorry! Let's just envy the little ones and let them enjoy their unique pair of mittens.

Children Sizes: Small, medium and large; mitten length (measured from cuff to tip of large claw) 5½", 6½" and 7½" (14 cm, 16.5 cm and 19 cm). To decide which size to knit, measure child's hand and add 2" (5 cm).

Yarn: 140 yards (128 m) of worsted weight yarn in red lobster color. Sample pair is knit with Morehouse Merino 3-Strand in Geranium Red.

Needles : Set of double-pointed US 4 or 5 (3.5 mm or 3.75 mm) or size to obtain gauge. You'll need 2 extra double-pointed needles, same size or smaller, as holding needles.

Gauge: 5 stitches = 1" (2.5 cm) over garter stitch.

Lobster Mitten is knit in two pieces. The claws are knit separately, beginning at the tips, then they are joined at the cuff.

SMALL CLAW

Cast on 3 stitches. Knit 1 row. Next: *knit first stitch, increase 1 stitch (increase by picking up yarn between stitches with left-hand needle, then knitting through back of loop over needle), knit to end of row. Repeat from * until you have 30 (34/38) stitches. Knit 2 more rows.

Divide stitches over two holding needles – 15 (17/19) stitches per needle. Break off yarn.

LARGE CLAW

Cast on 3 stitches. Knit 1 row. Next: *knit first stitch, increase 1 stitch (work increase same as for small claw), knit to end of row. Repeat from * until you have 30 (34/38) stitches. Now join stitches and start working in the round. Knit next row as follows: knit 8 (9/10) stitches, start with a new needle and knit the next 7 (8/9) stitches, start with a new needle and knit the next 7 (8/9) stitches, start with new needle and knit the remaining 8 (9/10) stitches. Join for knitting in the round and begin next round with first stitch on first needle: *purl 1 round, knit 1 round; repeat from * for a total of 13 (15/17) rounds – ending with a purl round.

COMBINING CLAWS

Now insert small claw into big claw so that the two claws are facing each other – the middle of the row on the small claw will be at the beginning of the round of the large claw (see illustration). Put the needles parallel to each other: the needle with the second half of the stitches on the small claw will be parallel to stitches on first and second needle on the large claw. Now knit the two claws together by knitting stitches from the big claw together with stitches from the small claw as follows: knit first stitch on big claw together with stitch on small claw (on small claw it will be the stitch after the middle); knit the two stitches together as one stitch (similar to three-needle bind-off – but without binding off stitches). Continue this way to end of round: knitting stitches on large claw together with stitches on small claw. You'll end up with a single set of 30 (34/38) stitches divided over 4 needles.

CUFF

*knit 4, knit 2 together; repeat from * to end of round, ending round with 0 (4/2) stitches. Knit 8 (10/11) rounds. Use yarn double for bind-off round and bind off loosely.

FINISHING

Sew each claw close from tip to where the two claws intersect with one another (pull the claws apart slightly). It will be easier to sew the claws on the right side – just sew them neatly by joining the edge stitches at each garter stitch ridge.

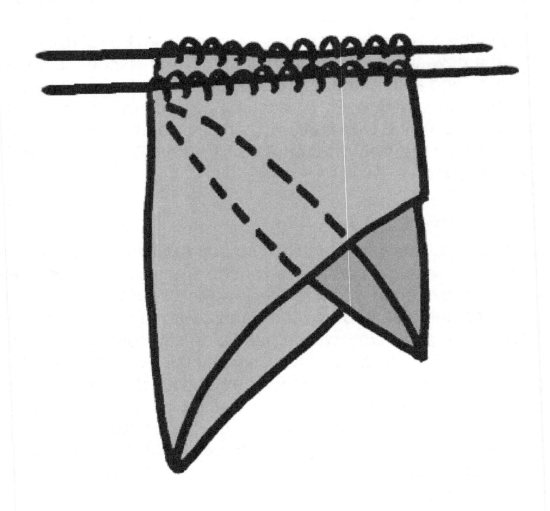

Lobster Tail Scarf

More lobstering going on! We've caught another one! Here is a short and sweet Scarf modeled after a lobster tail. It is, of course, the must-have accessory for the Lobster Claw Mittens, but it functions and looks perfectly well on its own and worn by adults – with or without additional nautical attire. And you can safely drop the lobster-red color!

You might want to stick with the length given in the pattern. There is a slit in one end of the Scarf to tuck in the other end. If you knit a longer version, you'll have to decide where to place that slit: up towards the neck or lower down, then adjust the pattern accordingly.

Size: About 40" long (101 cm) and 5" wide (12.7 cm).

Yarn: 225 yards (206 m) of sport weight yarn. Sample is knit with Morehouse Merino 2-Ply.

Needles: US 7 (4.5 mm) or size to obtain gauge.

Gauge: 18 stitches = 4" (10 cm) over pattern.

The Lobster Scarf has a slit, about 11" from cast-on edge, for inserting other end of Lobster Tail through, for a cozy wrap around the neck.

Cast on 48 stitches. Start 4x4 rib pattern as follows: *knit 4 stitches, purl 4 stitches; repeat from * to end of row. Work 15 rows in rib pattern. Next row: *knit 2 stitches together, knit the next 2 stitches together, purl 2 stitches together, and purl the next 2 stitches together; repeat from * to end of row = 24 stitches remaining. Start Scarf Pattern.

Scarf Pattern

Row 1 : knit.

Row 2 : purl.

Row 3 : knit.

Repeat these 3 rows for a total of 66 rows. Next, work row 1 and 2 of pattern, then work row 3 as follows: knit 8 stitches, bind off the next 8 stitches, then knit the remaining 8 stitches. Next, work Row 1 of pattern as follows: knit 8, cast on 8 stitches (using e-loop cast-on, see illustration in Panda Scarf Pattern), knit remaining 8 stitches.

Continue in Scarf Pattern, beginning with row 2, for another 199 rows, ending with row 2 of pattern. Next row: knit each stitch twice (worked as follows: knit stitch but don't drop stitch off left-hand needle, now knit into same stitch again but this time through the back of the stitch) = 48 stitches.

Finish Scarf with 15 rows in 4x4 rib pattern (same as beginning). Bind off in next row maintaining rib pattern.

FINISHING

Since this Scarf is knit with a large needle, soak it in warm water for a few minutes to get the full length. Then squeeze out as much water as possible and lay flat to dry, stretching Scarf to final length and width. Don't flatten tail fans at beginning and end of Scarf – just fan them out lightly.

Pony Tail Hat

If your hair is too short to sport a pony tail, this Hat might just do the job for a little fling and flicker of a tail. If you want an authentic version, match yarn color for Pony Tail with hair color and for a little extra flair, add braid bands or other hair accessory at the base of the tail.

Sizes: Child medium, child large (or adult small) and adult.

Yarn: Worsted weight yarn in 2 colors, 145 yards (133 m) for Hat, and a small amount for Pony Tail in a "hair" color. Sample is knit with Morehouse Merino 3-Strand.

Needles : Set of double-pointed US 5 or 6 (3.75 mm or 4.25 mm) or size to obtain gauge. You can start Hat using a 16" (40 cm) circular needle, then switch to double-pointed needles when circumference of Hat gets smaller towards tip. You'll also need a crochet hook size D or E (3.25 mm or 3.5 mm) for Pony Tail.

Notions : Stitch marker.

Gauge: 18 stitches = 4" (10 cm) over stockinette stitch.

With yarn color for Hat, cast on 72 (76/80) stitches. Make sure you use an elastic cast-on method (such as long-tail cast-on) and cast on loosely so edge will fit over head comfortably. The border is narrower than the rest of the Hat. Join for knitting in the round and mark beginning of round with stitch marker. Start 1x1 rib border worked as follows: *knit 1 stitch, purl 1 stitch; repeat from * to end of round. Work 10 (12/14) rounds in rib pattern.

Next round: knit and increase 8 stitches evenly – you now have a total of 80 (84/88) stitches. Knit until hat measures 4¼" (4½"/ 5") from cast-on edge (11 cm/11.5 cm/12.5 cm). Next, start decreases.

DECREASES

First decrease: *knit 6 stitches, knit 2 stitches together; repeat from * to end of round (*child large size only*: knit the last 4 stitches on this and the next 3 decrease rounds). Knit 6 rounds.

Second decrease: *knit 5 stitches, knit 2 stitches together; repeat from * to end of round. Knit 5 rounds.

Third decrease: *knit 4 stitches, knit 2 stitches together; repeat from * to end of round. Knit 4 rounds. Switch to double-pointed needles if you are using circular needle.

Fourth decrease: *knit 3 stitches, knit 2 stitches together; repeat from * to end of round. Knit 3 rounds.

Fifth decrease: *knit 2 stitches, knit 2 stitches together; repeat from * to end of round. Knit 2 rounds.

Sixth decrease: *knit 1 stitch, knit 2 stitches together; repeat from * to end of round. Knit 1 round.

Last decrease round: use yarn double for this last round of decreases (for extra strength – tail will be attached to these stitches): *knit 2 stitches together; repeat from * to end of round. Pull yarn through remaining stitches.

PONY TAIL

With contrasting yarn color cut 8 to 12 pieces 36" to 44" long (91 cm to 112 cm). Work each strand of tail as follows: fold piece of yarn in half and pull middle loop through top bind-off stitch using crochet hook. Now crochet chain stitch with yarn double – tail pieces should end up between 8" (20 cm) and 10" (25 cm) in length (crochet tightly so pieces will curl slightly). Pull yarn through last stitch and pull tight, then cut, leaving a short tuft. Add tail pieces to each bind-off stitch (and if you like a fuller pony tail, add more pieces and attach to yarn between stitches in bind-off round).

RatRace Scarf

Sometimes life feels like a rat race. Running around in circles, getting stressed out, burned out, hassled and frazzled. If that all sounds familiar, it's time to take a break and tune out with a little bit of knitting relaxation! Start a RatRace Scarf. And with each Rat you knit, stitch some of the day's frustrations off the needle and right into the Rats (they won't mind!). It's 8 easy ways to relieve stress. Keep knitting and if your life has been particularly hectic lately you just might end up with a RatRace Scarf a half a mile long (there are only 8 Rats in the original pattern). That's life!

Variations : Knit each Rat a different color with dazzling beads for eyes. White Rats seem to be popular with pet-rat owners and black ones with gleaming yellow eyes have been spotted around Halloween.

Size: About 56" (142 cm) long, not including the tail at one end; and 3½" wide (8.8 cm) at its full belly width (a little wider if you opt for the plumper Rat version).

Yarn: 230 yards (210 m) sport weight yarn. Sample is knit with Morehouse Merino Gator Yarn.

Other Materials : 16 beads for eyes, about ¼" in diameter (0.6 cm) and sewing thread for sewing bead eyes to faces.

Needles : Double-pointed US 5 or 6 (3.75 mm or 4.25 mm) or size to obtain gauge. Rats are knit back and forth, but you'll need an extra needle as holding needle.

Gauge: 5 stitches = 1" over garter stitch.

The RatRace Scarf is knit starting with the Rat at the head of the race and the second Rat is joined to the first one by knitting stitches from first Rat together with stitches from second one. There are a total of 8 Rats. The last Rat has a long tail.

HEAD OF FIRST RAT

Cast on 3 stitches and knit 2 rows.

Rows 3 & 4: knit 1, increase 1 stitch (work increases throughout pattern as follows: pick up yarn between stitches with left-hand needle, then knit through back of loop over needle), knit to end of row.

Rows 5 & 6: knit.

Repeat rows 3 through 6 until you have 13 stitches, ending with 2 knit rows.

EARS

Row 1: knit 1, increase 1 stitch, knit 1, increase 1, knit 9, increase 1, knit 1, increase 1, knit last stitch = 17 stitches.

Rows 2, 4, 6 & 8: knit.

Row 3: knit 1, increase 1, knit 3, increase 1, knit 9, increase 1, knit 3, increase 1, knit last stitch = 21 stitches.

Row 5: knit 1, increase 1, knit 5, increase 1, knit 9, increase 1, knit 5, increase 1, knit last stitch = 25 stitches.

Row 7: knit 1, increase 1, knit 7, increase 1, knit 9, increase 1, knit 7, increase 1, knit last stitch = 29 stitches.

Row 9: knit 2, bind off 8 (count stitches as you are binding them off, not as you are knitting them), knit 9 (includes stitch on needle from last bind-off stitch), bind off 8, knit last 2 stitches (again, includes stitch on needle from last bind-off stitch) = 13 stitches remaining. This is what stitches look like on needle: 2 stitches, then a hole where you bind off 8, 9 stitches, another hole from bind-off, and the final 2 stitches.

Row 10: knit row and pull yarn tight between bind-off stitches.

Row 11: knit row to last 2 stitches, knit those 2 stitches together = 12 stitches.

Row 12: repeat row 11 = 11 stitches.

Row 13: knit 1, increase 1, knit to end of row = 12 stitches.

Rows 14-16: repeat row 13 (you'll end up with 15 stitches).

For a slightly plumper Rat, repeat row 13 until you have 19 stitches.

BODY
Knit 22 rows.

Next: *knit row to last 2 stitches, knit the 2 stitches together; repeat from * until you have 9 stitches remaining. Knit 1 more row (yarn will be at left on right-side row). Break off yarn leaving a 6" tail. Leave stitches on needle.

SECOND RAT
Start with a new needle and begin next Rat.

Cast on 3 stitches and knit 2 rows. Then repeat rows 3 through 6 for Head until you have 9 stitches, ending with 1 knit row and yarn at left on right-side row. Now you'll be joining the first Rat with this second on. Put needles parallel to each other – ready to knit rows – with first rat facing you (wrong side) and beginning of second rat behind first one (see illustration). Now knit stitches from first Rat together with stitches from second Rat: knit first stitch on needle closest to you together with first stitch on needle inback, knit them as one stitch; then knit second stitch on needle closest to you together with second stitch on needle in back; etc.

Tip: for the first 3 stitches use yarn tail from first rat together with yarn on second rat – this saves having to darn in the end of yarn later on.

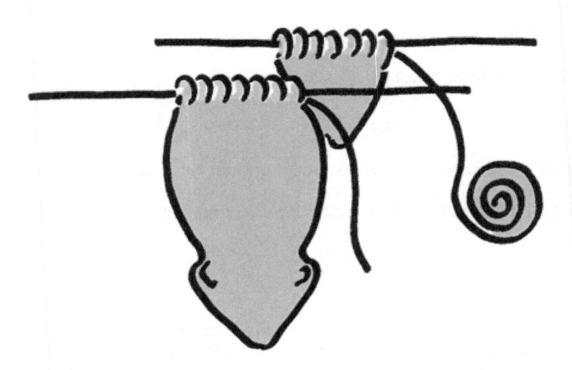

FINISH SECOND RAT

Continue with head on second Rat: repeat rows 3 through 6 until you have 13 stitches. Finish Ears and Body the same way as on first Rat.

THE NEXT 6 RATS

Then start with next Rat and continue this way until you have 8 Rats. Work body on last Rat as follows: knit the 22 rows for body. Next: *knit row to last 2 stitches, knit those 2 stitches together; repeat from * until you have 4 stitches left.

TAIL ON LAST RAT

The last Rat is the only one with a tail. Work tail as I-cord: knit the 4 stitches; instead of turning knitting, slide stitches to other end of needle and knit the 4 stitches again in same stitch sequence (pull yarn tight between last and first stitch). Repeat this row until tail measures 4" (10 cm). Next: knit first stitch, knit 2 stitches together, knit last stitch and repeat I-cord procedure until entire tail measures about 7" (18 cm). Pull yarn through stitches.

Sew bead eyes to heads (below ears) with sewing thread.

Rooster Hat

Attracting attention, chasing chicks, crowing way too early in the morning and strutting around are a rooster's main functions (I'm very familiar with their activities – we've got several dozens of them at Morehouse Farm). And this Hat with its bright red spikes is definitely an attention-grabbing top (other functions optional). But wearing it calls for some pretty cool moves on the slope or a purposeful strut through town après ski.

Sizes: Child and adult.

Yarn: 150 yards (137 m) of worsted weight yarn for Hat, about 100 yards (90 m) of sport weight yarn in red for the comb of the rooster. Sample is knit Morehouse Merino 3-Strand for Hat, and 2-Ply for comb.

Needles : For Hat US 4 or 5 (3.5 mm or 3.75 mm) or size to obtain gauge; for comb 24" (40 cm) circular and set of double-pointed US 3 or 4 (3.25 mm or 3.5 mm).

Gauge: 18 stitches = 4" (10 cm) over garter stitch for Hat, 6 stitches = 1 inch over stockinette stitch for comb.

Hat is knit in two halves (two half-rounds). Then stitches are picked up along the rounded sides of both halves and then knit together to shape the tips of the comb. Start with yarn color for Hat and cast on 38 (42) stitches for first half of Hat. Knit 42 (46) rows.

DECREASES FOR SHAPING HAT

First decrease: *this first decrease applies to adult size only* : knit 5 stitches, knit 2 stitches together; *knit 6 stitches, knit 2 together;

repeat from * to end of row, ending row with knit 3 = total of 37 stitches remaining. Knit 5 rows.

Continue as follows: (*start decreases for child with this second decrease; for adult size continue with this next decrease*)

Second decrease: knit 4 stitches, knit 2 together; *knit 5 stitches, knit 2 together; repeat from * to end of row, ending row with knit 4 (3) = total of 33 (32) stitches. Knit 5 rows.

Third decrease: knit 3 stitches, knit 2 together; *knit 4 stitches, knit 2 together; repeat from * to end of row, ending row with knit 4 (3) = total of 28 (27) stitches. Knit 5 rows.

Fourth decrease: knit 2 stitches, knit 2 together; *knit 3 stitches, knit 2 together; repeat from * to end of row, ending row with knit 3 (4) = total 23 (22) stitches. Knit 3 rows.

Fifth decrease: knit 1 stitch, knit 2 together; *knit 2 stitches, knit 2 together; repeat from * to end of row, ending row with knit 0 (3) = total of 17 stitches. Knit 3 rows.

Sixth decrease: knit 2 together; *knit 1 stitch, knit 2 together; repeat from * to end of row = total of 11 stitches. Knit 1 row.

Seventh decrease: *knit 2 together; repeat from * to end of row, knit last stitch = 6 stitches. Put stitches on stitch holder or holding needle (use a needle from set of double-pointed needles).

Make second half of Hat the same way as first half.

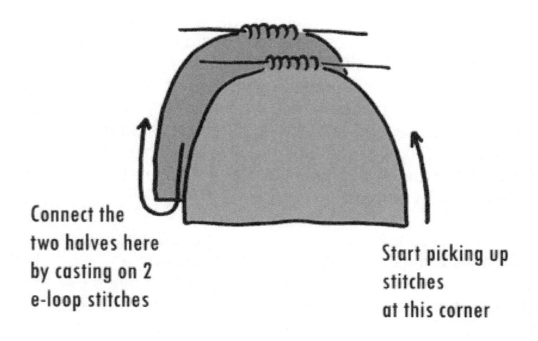

Connect the two halves here by casting on 2 e-loop stitches

Start picking up stitches at this corner

COMB

You'll now combine the two halves by picking up stitches along rounded sides of both halves (see illustration). Use circular needle and red sport weight yarn for comb and pick up stitches on first half as follows: right side facing you, start at cast-on edge and pick up 1 stitch at cast-on edge, then pick up 1 stitch per 2 rows to top of hat. Knit the 6 stitches on holding needle and pick up stitches along other side towards cast-on edge. Pick up 1 stitch at cast-on edge. Now cast on 2 stitches using e-loop cast-on method using e-loop cast-on (see illustration in Panda Scarf Pattern on how to work e-loop cast-on), then start picking up stitches on second half the same way as on first half. The hats are now connected by the 2 e-loop stitches. Finish second half by casting on 2 stitches. You should have 74 (84) stitches per side (including 2 e-loop stitches per side) for a total of 148 (168) stitches on needle. Now join round by knitting stitches beginning with picked-up stitches on first half. Knit 2 rounds.

COMB TIPS

For first tip, put the first 7 stitches (use the last e-loop stitch as your first stitch so comb tips will be centered) on one of the double-pointed needles and the last 7 stitches (including the first e-loop stitch) from circular needle on a second needle. You'll work with just 3 needles – the stitches will be on 2 needles and you'll use the 3rd needle to knit with – it will be a little awkward at first but it's easier knitting than dividing stitches over 3 needles. Work tips as follows: *Knit 1 round. Knit second round to last 2 stitches, knit those 2 stitches together. Third round: knit the first 2 stitches together, knit to end of round. Repeat from * until you have 2 stitches left. Pull yarn through. Break off yarn.

Next comb tip: re-attach yarn and use the next 8 stitches at beginning of round together with the last 8 stitches and work tip the same as first one. For each subsequent tip, add 1 stitch per side of tip until you reach 12 stitches per side; then finish adult size hat with tips that are 10, 9 and 8 stitches; and child size with 9 and 8.

Printed in Great Britain
by Amazon

37235814R00084